HE MOVED A MOUNTAIN

He Moved a
MOUNTAIN

THE LIFE OF FRANK CALDER AND THE
NISGA'A LAND CLAIMS ACCORD

JOAN HARPER

RONSDALE PRESS

RONSDALE PRESS
3350 West 21st Avenue
Vancouver, B.C. Canada V6S 1G7
www.ronsdalepress.com

Typesetting: Julie Cochrane, in Granjon 11.5 pt on 15
Cover Design: Julie Cochrane
Paper: Ancient Forest Friendly 70lb Envirographic 100, FSC Recycled,
    100% post-consumer waste, totally chlorine-free and acid-free

Ronsdale Press wishes to thank the following for their support of its publishing program: the Canada Council for the Arts, the Government of Canada through the Canada Book Fund, the British Columbia Arts Council, and the Province of British Columbia through the British Columbia Book Publishing Tax Credit program.

Library and Archives Canada Cataloguing in Publication

Harper, Joan
    He moved a mountain : the life of Frank Calder and the Nisga'a land claims accord / Joan Harper.

Includes bibliographical references and index.
ISBN 978-1-55380-227-3 (print)
ISBN 978-1-55380-228-0 (ebook) / 978-1-55380-229-7 (pdf)

    1. Calder, Frank, 1915–2006. 2. Politicians — British Columbia — Biography.
3. Businessmen — British Columbia — Biography. 4. Niska Indians — British
Columbia — Biography. 5. Niska Indians — British Columbia — Claims.
6. Indians — Kings and rulers — Biography. I. Title.

FC3828.1.C34H37 2013   971.1'04092   C2013-900949-3

At Ronsdale Press we are committed to protecting the environment. To this end we are working with Canopy and printers to phase out our use of paper produced from ancient forests. This book is one step towards that goal.

Printed in Canada by Island Blue, Victoria, B.C.

To the memory of
Frank Arthur Calder,
his Calder and Clark families,
the Nisga'a First Nation,
and all First Nation
people everywhere

ACKNOWLEDGEMENTS

He Moved a Mountain was a difficult book to research. Frank Calder's career as an MLA encompassed the years from 1949 to 1979, but the BC legislature did not begin *Hansard*, the official report of proceedings in the house, until 1970. By this time the major projects of his life had been accomplished. This has made a necessary reliance on newspaper articles, archives and memories of living relatives and friends for much of the information concerning his life.

There are a great many people to whom I owe a debt of thanks for their assistance. First and foremost I want to thank Tamaki Calder. Frank's wife very much wants his story told and was extremely helpful in providing me with Frank's photos and scrapbooks, and in relating conversations she had with Frank as well as many interesting happenings in their life together. Frank's brother Phillip Clark was also of great assistance. He had shared Frank's early years and attended Coqualeetza Residential School with his brother and provided many anecdotes. His sister Dorothy Smith (Clark), who has since passed away, along with her daughter Barbara Smart provided me with photographs and articles they had kept. Her granddaughter Rhonda Westra has thoroughly researched and compiled an extensive family tree of the Calder/Clark ancestors to which she provided me access. I am grateful to all Frank's wonderful family.

There are others without whose help this book could not have been written. I want to thank Major General (retired) David Wightman who gave liberally of his time by reading drafts, editing and making useful suggestions throughout the time of my early efforts. When I was almost ready to give up he prevented me by saying I had done too much work to quit now. Next I need to thank Professor Hamar Foster of the Faculty of Law at the University of Victoria. He very kindly read the first two chapters and corrected errors I had made in the history as well as relating his relationship with Frank. Jim Hume, columnist with the Victoria *Times Colonist*, was a close friend of Frank's. He not only answered questions but also spent time reading an early draft. He commented that the political perspective was correct and that he had been there every step of the way as a political reporter covering the legislature. The librarians at the Victoria Public Library were extremely helpful and answered questions as well as arranging a video showing of the National Film Board's feature on Frank Calder: *Time Immemorial: As Long as Rivers Flow*. Finally, I must thank my long-suffering husband who put up with me and my many frustrations during the time I was writing this book. He made trips to the legislative library and the archives to check facts for me and never seemed to lose patience.

Contents

Introduction

DOCTOR FRANK ARTHUR CALDER was one of Canada's greatest Canadians. He was Nisga'a, born in 1915 in the remote Nass River Valley of northern British Columbia. His people, the Nisga'a, were passionate about their land and, from the 1880s, when they heard rumours that a reserve system was being contemplated, the nation had fought to keep possession of their traditional lands. They soon discovered that attaining legal title would demand enormous struggle and persistence. As attempt after attempt failed, they came to describe the process to be as difficult as "moving a mountain." As a young child Frank Calder showed promise, and at a great feast his chieftain father charged him with the task of moving the mountain to gain Nisga'a land title.

From his early years with all the disadvantages of living in a remote area with few opportunities, Frank rose to gain a university education and to serve as a member of the Legislature of British Columbia for twenty-six years. His path was never easy, but in spite of many difficulties his determination and dedication to the task with which he had been charged never wavered. He fought not only for the land claims of his people but also for justice on numerous issues that affected all his constituents who lived in northern Canada, Aboriginal and Caucasian alike. Educational opportunities, good jobs and government services in the north were often unequal to those in the south. His principles of fairness for all remained constant even when he faced strong opposition from his own political party and at times even from his own people.

The pinnacle of his career was his success in bringing the issue of Aboriginal land title to the opinion of the Canadian courts. Even though the question had never been brought to any court in any country, he believed there was precedent for it in English law. His efforts culminated in three court battles, but it was not until it reached the Supreme Court of Canada, where a split decision was handed down, that Parliament, in an all-party vote, was convinced to pass the law that recognized Aboriginal land title in Canada. The court's decision had not been a victory, but parliament made it one and changed the course of history, not only in Canada but also in many countries where Aboriginal peoples reside. The debate in the Supreme Court of Canada will ever be known as the "Calder Case."

Although this biographer never met Frank personally, after more than three years of research and interviews with his family and friends, she believes that she has come to know and understand him well. Her research into his life and work has filled her with the greatest admiration for him and his achievements (see appendix 1 for a list of his honours and awards). Throughout his life he always upheld the principles that he believed were right even if they harmed his career or offended fellow chiefs. The unfolding of his life story serves as an inspiration to all.

CHAPTER 1

The Early Years

ON AUGUST 3, 1915, in the Nass River Valley of northern British Columbia, Dr. Frank Arthur Calder was born. He was a Nisga'a, which means "people of the Nass." His family had lived there for generation upon generation and had been involved in the traditional tribal leadership of the nation. His family lineage is somewhat complicated and merits a brief discussion. His birth parents were Emily Leask Clark and Job Clark, who was the nephew of the Nisga'a chief, Arthur Calder, who bore the title Na-qua-oon, translated as Chief Long Arm. It was the traditional title of the chief of the Nisga'a who presided over the village of Greenville. Frank's mother's sister, Louisa Leask Calder, was married to Arthur Calder.

Frank Calder's birth was steeped in a mythical dream. Almost two years earlier, Louisa and Chief Arthur Calder had lost twin sons. One had died at birth and the other before reaching his first birthday. Louisa and Arthur were devastated. With no prospect of future pregnancies, Louisa lapsed into a lingering depression from which it seemed nothing could rouse her. Then one day in Gingolx (Kincolith), a village near the mouth of the Nass River where it empties into the Pacific Ocean below the Alaskan border, an old woman from the Frog clan had a vivid dream. To her it was so real that she paddled all the way up the river to visit the chief and his wife in Greenville.

She met with Louisa and described her dream in vivid detail. She said it was so life-like that she believed it must be true. The dream, the woman said, foretold that Louisa's sister Emily would become pregnant and that the child would be a boy and would have the soul of Louisa's first twin and the spirit of chief Na-qua-oon. The old woman insisted that Louisa and Arthur must adopt this child. The dream instilled hope in the child-less couple. Upon hearing the news, they immediately related it to Emily and Job Clark. Soon afterwards, Emily did indeed become pregnant and the Clarks agreed that if Emily's child proved to be a son Louisa and Arthur Calder would adopt him.

That summer, Emily followed her husband Job along with other fam-ilies to the river's mouth to work at Mill Bay. There, almost twenty-five years earlier in 1881, a cannery had been built by the British Columbia Fishing and Packing Company, which later became Canada Packers. The cannery provided good seasonal jobs that were well paid while the fishing lasted. It was here while she and her husband were working in Nass Harbour that Emily gave birth. The child was a boy — as the woman from Gingolx had predicted. True to their word, Emily and Job Clark gave the child over to the Calders in a traditional Nisga'a adoption ceremony. Before doing so, however, they bestowed the name Frank upon him — after Job's father. The Calders gave him the second name of Arthur, his adoptive father's name and also that of his adoptive grand-father.[1]

Frank's adoption was possible within the Nisga'a because Emily and Louisa were sisters and had the same crest, that of the killer whale. The Nisga'a Nation has four clans or *wilps*, the Gisk'aast (Killer Whale), the Laxgibuu (Wolf), the Laxsgiik (Eagle) and the Kao'a or Skawah (Frog or Raven). At birth every baby receives the crest of his or her mother and keeps it for life. It is forbidden for any person to marry someone with the same crest. The preservation of the marriage prohibition is the reason no child can be adopted by a mother with a different crest from the one with which he or she was born. Children always have the same crest as their mother so adoption to a mother with a different crest would change the crest of the child and interfere with the prohibition.

Frank Calder was born a Clark, but he retained his adoptive name of Frank Arthur Calder throughout his life. Yet he was not entirely separated from his birth parents, for, in the Nisga'a tradition, cousins whose mothers are sisters are raised almost as if they are brothers and sisters. Frank spent time in both households, and it was not until he was grown up that he learned he had been adopted. It was a large family group. Louisa and the chief adopted one other child, a girl named Bertha, and Frank's birth parents had eight children in all.

Upon Frank's adoptive father's death, his birth father Job Clark became Chief Long Arm. Nisga'a chieftainship passes to the eldest nephew. Job was the eldest nephew through his mother's side of the family.

The Nisga'a land into which Frank was born was a wilderness of extreme beauty, wild and free. The Nass, flowing from the mountains to the sea, is some 378 kilometres long and with its tributaries has a basin of nearly 13,000 square kilometres. The evergreen trees — Douglas fir, Sitka spruce, hemlock and red and yellow cedar — are huge, the ocean to the west vast and the people few. The region ranges from wide beaches to deep fjords to glaciers and snow-capped mountains. Even though it is situated in the far north of BC, the Nass valley has a surprisingly moderate climate, warmed by the Japanese current. The sea life is lavish and bountiful.

Over the years the Nisga'a people had built four villages along the Nass: Gingolx (Kincolith) near the mouth; Laxgalts'ap (Greenville), where Frank Calder grew up; New Aiyansh, where the totem poles are located, and farthest from the mouth; Gitwinkaihlkw (Canyon City). Together they had developed their own culture and traditions. Their intricately carved totems told historical tales and depicted their deep spiritual belief of being connected to the world around them.

Frank's people had lived along the Nass River with their own way of life intact for thousands of years, or "from time immemorial" as the Nisga'a elders described it. By the time Frank was born, however, there had been a period of over a hundred years during which European explorers and traders had begun to transform the Nisga'a culture. The first to arrive, somewhat farther north, were two Russian ships in 1745, led by Vitus Bering in the *St. Peter* and Alexei Chirikov in the *St. Paul*.² Chirikov landed on Prince of Wales Island, now part of Alaska, only a little over a hundred kilometres from the mouth of the Nass River. Bering died on Kayak Island, but survivors from his expedition reported sighting Mount St. Elias, now part of Canada's territory in the Yukon. More importantly for the future, they began trading with First Nations people, but exactly which nations they contacted remains unclear.

The furs with which the Russians returned were so highly prized that subsequently the Russians set up trading posts on what is now the Alaskan panhandle,³ close to the present towns of Ketchikan and Sitka.⁴ Eventually they had trading posts as far south as California. Along with the Russians, Spanish ships visited the West Coast, but none of the Spaniards ventured as far north as the Nass.

News of the abundance of furs to be found in the northwest region of America slowly filtered across Russia, throughout Europe and to Great Britain. In 1794 a British maritime trader, Charles Bishop, stopped at the mouth of the Nass River, and commented, "It is a doubt with us, wither these People had ever seen a Vessel before. They wore by far, the most savage wild appearance I have ever seen."⁵ Whether he considered them savage or not, Bishop liked their furs. He returned to Britain with a fortune in pelts, shared by his investors and crew members, and thereafter a lively if sporadic trade developed with the Nisga'a and surrounding nations.

In the 1830s, the Hudson's Bay Company, lured by accounts of the profitable trade to be had on the coast, decided to set up a regular route to service the region. The company was so convinced by reports of the region's riches that they ordered the building of a ship in Britain specifically for the purpose. Launched in 1835, it was christened the *Beaver* and sailed to Fort Vancouver on the Columbia River. Thereafter it plied its trade up and down the coast of BC and made frequent stops at the mouth of the Nass. It conducted trade with the Nisga'a and their neighbouring First Nations — the Gitxsan, the Kwakiutl and the Tsimshian as well as others. It was the first regular contact these nations had with Europeans.[6]

The *Beaver* was destined to play an important role in the history of Frank Calder's adoptive family. One of the *Beaver*'s deck hands was a man named Arthur Calder. Over time, during numerous calls at the Nass, Calder met a Nisga'a princess nicknamed Queen Victoria. This was because in profile she was said to resemble the Queen. They were married and had several children, the first of whom was a boy named Arthur after his father. In due course the child became Chief Na-qua-oon.

Frank's birth father was the son of a Scot, Frank Roundy. Roundy was a colourful individual who arrived in the Nass River valley in the late 1890s with a fellow prospector. They had heard of a minor gold rush at American Creek and set off hoping to make their fortune. Roundy did not find gold in the Nass, but during his time there he met and married an Aboriginal woman from Hazelton, Ellen Wale, and fathered one son, Frank's birth father, Job. Discouraged at not finding gold, Roundy, shortly after his son's birth, left to search for the yellow metal even farther north — deserting his wife and his son.

After his father left, Job Roundy was adopted and raised in the community of Greenville by Anglican missionaries.[7] Like many Nisga'a, Job was given the surname of the missionaries who adopted him, and even after he became chief was known as Job Clark. As a boy, the missionaries sent him to Alert Bay Indian Mission School for his education. When he became an adult he worked as a fisherman, and in 1912 he married Emily Leask in Port Simpson. Emily was only fifteen years old at the time, and she had been educated at the well-known Crosby girls' school there. She was married in Port Simpson because she wanted to be married in the chapel of the school she had attended. She could speak English well, and later in life became the radio operator for the area, advising fishing fleets and other small transport of weather conditions. Some years after her marriage, she gave birth to her third child, Frank, whom she gave up for adoption. Although both Frank's grandfathers were European, their marriages had been to Nisga'a women, and all four of his parents were Nisga'a, which made Frank a "status Indian."

When traders from Europe began to trade regularly with the First Nations people at ports on the coast of British Columbia, it did not mean that trade was a new concept to the people of the region. For centuries the Nisga'a had traded with the Gitxsan, the Kwakiutl (now Kwakwaka'wakw), the Tsimshian and even nations as far away as the Haida. But trade with the Hudson's Bay Company was different. The newcomers had goods the Nisga'a had never encountered before: sharp steel knives, matches, coloured beads for sewing, metal hooks for fishing and, above all, rifles for hunting. The Nisga'a were delighted to trade their plentiful pelts for such articles. From their point of view the European traders were getting the worst of the deal. Value is always relative, and pelts were plentiful to the Nisga'a and the traders' goods scarce.

Quickly following the traders to the region were Christian missionaries. They represented many denominations, but those who first set up a mission at the mouth of the Nass were Church of England (Anglican). It was to become the dominant religion of the Nisga'a Nation, and the faith to which Frank Calder would remain loyal throughout his life.

Reverend Robert Tomlinson founded the first Anglican mission at Kincolith. Palmer Patterson, of the Department of History at the University of Waterloo, offers an interesting account of the first decade. He relates tales that reveal the progression of the relations between the church and the native community. Soon after the missionaries arrived around the year 1870, Tomlinson accidentally set fire to a chief's orchard. Fruit trees were highly prized, and even though Tomlinson paid recompense, the chief never forgave him.[8] In spite of such initial setbacks, however, it did not take long before the missionaries became an integral part of Nisga'a life. The Nisga'a even began to copy the style of the missionaries' housing.

Calder's ancestors would have occupied traditional Nisga'a longhouses that were constructed with massive cedar posts and beams with moveable vertical wallboards set into grooved timbers top and bottom. The house of the chief was always much larger than others and had a fire pit in the centre with broad steps leading down to it from the main floor of the dwelling. The steps were wide in order that they could be used for meal preparation or other domestic activities. Split cedar planks were used for roofs to keep out the rain.[9] The missionaries desired a different more European style of home.

To accomplish this, in 1876 they established a sawmill at Kincolith and began to build houses in a familiar European design. The natives began to see the new style as superior and referred to them as "Christian housing." Many Nisga'a wanted to occupy such a house but it was beyond the means of all but the most privileged. The chiefs were the first to live in such homes.

As a chief's son, Frank would have grown up in a European style house built from sawn lumber and separated into rooms and covered by a steep roof of solid, cedar shakes that would keep the snow off in winter. By today's standards it would be considered Spartan; the indoor areas consisted of little more than a living room, a good sized kitchen and two small bedrooms. It was probably heated by a cookstove in contrast to those of most Nisga'a who might have a makeshift heater made from an oil barrel or an open fire-pit with the smoke drifting out through a hole in the ceiling. Many Nisga'a still lived in log dwellings of no more than a single room. Nearby many had a potato patch and a few boasted fruit trees, mainly apple. Neither the European style housing nor the traditional Nisga'a style had running water or electricity and furnishings would have been minimal.

Soon after settling in the area, the missionaries began to minister to the sick, hold church services and Sunday school classes, and set up schools. The Nisga'a came to look upon them as a necessity to the well-being of their nation. Patterson tells of one occasion when the missionary at Kincolith left on sabbatical. When no replacement was forthcoming, the Nisga'a sent a letter of complaint to the bishop in Victoria.[10] Eventually, almost all Nisga'a were baptized and after baptism took a name that was European in origin.

The missionaries brought benefits but they also caused a negative impact on Nisga'a culture. They believed and therefore preached that Nisga'a myths, creeds and customs were heathen and should be expunged. In their zeal they did not recognize that their standards and attitudes were harmful and were causing identity problems in the Nisga'a. They took away native respect for long-standing moral beliefs and negated the value of their beautiful arts.

Joe Gosnell, a future chief who would prove instrumental in the Nisga'a land claim negotiations, aptly described this in *Spirit Dance at Meziadin*. Here he tells of his experience as a child when playing around the houses of the missionaries and chiefs, where he found intricately carved beams:

> Playing in the crawl space under his grandfather's house in Gitwinksi-hlkw, the young Joseph Gosnell did not understand why anyone would carve such beautiful figures on dusty wooden beams. It was only years later . . . that he realized the foundations of his grandfather's house had once been the towering Nisga'a totem poles that graced the main street of the remote village [New Aiyansh]."[11]

Like other First Nations, the Nisga'a continue to struggle with the legacy of the missionaries and to negotiate their Christian faith with the recovery of their suppressed culture. Frank, while Christian, remained deeply committed to the traditions of his people. When he eventually married, he insisted on an Anglican Church wedding in Greenville, followed some months later by a traditional ceremony to adopt his wife into a Nisga'a clan.

———∞∞∞———

Frank's parents, both by birth and adoption spoke English because they had attended schools run and funded by missionaries. His birth father had been sent to Port Alberni and his birth mother to Port Simpson. To help their children learn English even when they were very young, they had them attend the mission school in Greenville. The quality of instruction in these mission schools was often not very high. Frank's brother Phillip Clark, who now lives in Prince Rupert, recalls the school in Greenville as not being much help to him. He commented, "Most of the time I didn't have a clue as to what was going on."

A more effective method of learning English for both Frank and

Phillip came from the storeowner at Mill Bay, Mr. Donaldson. The Donaldsons had built a house with a yard surrounded by a six-foot fence where their two sons and daughter, Graham, Colly and Christine, played. Frank and Phillip were invited by Mr. Donaldson to play with his sons inside the fenced yard. Graham and Colly spoke English and perhaps a few words of Nisga'a, and soon they all learned to converse easily with each other. One day as they were playing, Phillip remembers Mr. Donaldson asking them what they wanted to be when they grew up and recalls saying, "a crab fisherman." Graham immediately replied, "a business man." Colly piped up and said, "a hobo." Mr. Donaldson was so angry at his son's reply that Frank never got to say a word.

Arthur Calder, chief Na-qua-oon, had a special purpose in raising Frank. He saw great potential in his adopted son and hoped the young boy would grow to be a leader for his people in their struggle for land title. He believed if he made him a responsible child he would grow into a responsible man capable of correcting the many injustices Aboriginals faced. Arthur gave his son tasks that helped him identify with the land as their land. He asked him to carry fresh water to the house several times a day, beginning in the early morning. He also sent him into the woods to gather wood for the fire and taught him to hunt. Frank grew up knowing that title to Nisga'a lands was a serious issue, and one that had to be remedied.

During the years that Frank was a young child, the only treaties that had been signed with First Nations people in British Columbia were the fourteen treaties negotiated by Sir James Douglas, governor of the colony of Vancouver Island from 1851 to 1864. However, subsequent colonial policy makers refused to honour the treaties and denied that Aboriginal land title had ever existed. They alleged that First Nations people were too primitive to understand a claim to territory. In 1871, when British Columbia joined Canada, Aboriginal land title was not included in the agreement, and thus did not, apparently, exist in law.

The year of 1876 marked the passage of the first Canadian Indian Act

— the act that Frank would spend most of his life fighting against. It stated a policy of protection, assimilation and Christianization of the First Nation peoples. Not only would they be denied title to land but areas of hunting and fishing would be severely limited. The government would decide land borders for reserves, and all Aboriginal people would gradually be relocated to live within them. The remaining bulk of their land would then be subdivided and sold to settlers. The money received from sales would cover the costs of administering the reserves and provide for small annual payments for residents of the reserves.

In addition, the government promised that health care and education would be provided to Aboriginals, but neither the health nor the education services supplied were of the quality the general population received. Schools for Aboriginals only went to grade ten, and they often had to travel long distances to find medical care. Alcohol consumption was also outlawed for Aboriginals, and later amendments suppressed numerous First Nation practices, including the potlatch on the coast of British Columbia and the sun dance on the prairies. Frank grew up understanding these grievances and in adult life his goal would always be to eliminate the paternalistic and condescending Indian Act and its system of reserves in order to return to self-governance and self-determination for his people, and all First Nations.[12]

Frank's nation, the Nisga'a, had historically hunted, fished and trapped over the entire Nass River basin. They had never signed a treaty with Douglas and knew little of the Indian Act. It was not until the early 1880s that the Calders' forebears became aware that the politicians in Victoria believed that the Nisga'a had no inherent right to their land. They did not accept this concept easily. In *Let Right Be Done*, Frank related the following story about an event that took place almost two years before Commissioner Riley arrived on the Nisga'a lands and finally succeeded in setting the Nisga'a reserve boundaries:

> One summer day, the Nisga'a were gathered on the bank of the Nass River. The adults were chatting and fishing and the children were playing when five white men suddenly appeared on the opposite bank. The Nisga'a watched as they set up something the Nisga'a had never seen before and through which they seemed to be looking; a tripod of sorts. Curi-

ous, a canoe with several braves crossed and in Chinook asked what they were doing. The men replied that the instrument through which they looked would set a boundary on the South and East sides of the river and that they would be given all the land inside it. The braves returned and reported to the chief what they had been told. The next morning every canoe the Nisga'a owned was filled with braves and every brave carried a Hudson's Bay musket. They crossed the river to where the surveyors camped.

The surveyors led by Captain William Jemmett were just starting to cook breakfast when canoes packed with over a hundred braves arrived. They landed with a chorus of cries, "Get off our land." Not a single Nisga'a wanted anything to do with boundaries. Vastly outnumbered the surveyors had little choice but to pack up and leave.[13]

As they watched the white men scatter, the Nisga'a believed they had seen the last of such surveyors.

Later in 1887, a Royal Commission was struck to look into the incident. The Honourable Peter O'Reilly, a gold commissioner, county court judge and member of the first legislative council of British Columbia, was chosen to survey boundaries for reserves throughout British Columbia. He dutifully set out from his home on Ellice Point in Victoria to perform his task. As well as surveying the boundaries of the reserves, he was to explain clearly to the Nisga'a, along with other nations, that they must now live within the boundaries that the government set for them.[14]

The Nisga'a were astounded when O'Reilly arrived in their territory and said that he would be surveying boundaries for their land and that the Queen would give them all the land within the new borders. They laughed and wondered out loud, "Why would she give us more land when we don't need any more?" But when O'Reilly and his crew set about staking the ground and emphatically explained that all Nisga'a people would be required to live within these borders, their laughter turned to anger. Their chief complained, "We understand 'land.' We do not understand 'reserve.' We have no word for 'reserve' only 'land' ... 'our land.'"[15]

When Frank was only six years old, chief Na-qua-oon took him to a great feast at Gingolx (Kincolith) where the Nisga'a people from all the clans up and down the river had gathered. Tables had been prepared laden with smoked seal, roasted game and dried salmon. There were mixtures of seaweed and oolichan oil into which to dip the fish, along with many varieties of shellfish.

As the evening wore on, the chiefs and elders began to discuss land claims and reminisced about earlier attempts to regain land that had been confiscated from them. As early as 1890, the Nisga'a had established a committee to address their land rights. Over the years they had sent delegations to Victoria, Ottawa and on one occasion in 1906 all the way to London, England. In 1913 they hired the firm of Fox and Preece in London to serve a petition to the British Crown in an attempt to have their rights recognized. For all legal matters they hired competent lawyers, some of whom believed in the cause and worked for very low fees but all efforts came to naught. The hearings supported the belief that they had no rights to the land except to occupy the reserve that had been granted to them. The chiefs described the problem as "an immovable mountain."

Late in the evening, Frank, sitting with his family, was picked up by his father and stood on the table. In a loud voice the chief proclaimed, "This boy, this dream boy, I am going to send to a white area. He will learn the ways of the white man, he will speak like a white man, eat like a white man and walk like a white man." Then, pointing at the mountain so Frank would look at it, he proclaimed: "He will move that mountain."

CHAPTER 2

Schooling

CHIEF NA-QUA-OON took seriously the task of raising Frank to know and understand the ways of the white man. Three years after he had made the pledge to the gathering of chiefs to bring up Frank to understand the thinking and habits of the non-native population, he sent Frank to Coqualeetza residential school in Sardis. Frank had just turned nine years old. The year was 1924, and Coqualeetza was still a Methodist mission school. Universal government residential schooling would not be established in BC for another four years.

Schooling in Canada is a provincial responsibility, and in British Columbia in 1873 the province imposed compulsory school attendance for all children.[1] However, the regulation did not apply to Aboriginals because the province did not have jurisdiction over them. First Nations were a federal responsibility. Not until 1920 did the federal government pass a law, reinforcing a largely ignored law passed much earlier in 1882, mandating that First Nations children were to attend school.[2]

Eight years later in 1928, many federal residential schools for First

Nations were established in British Columbia, as they already had been in many parts of Canada. They were funded by the Department of Indian Affairs and operated by churches, both Protestant and Catholic. The schools had been founded in the belief that education would help First Nations children bridge the gap between life on the reserves and the outside, modern world. It was with the hope that the children who attended would be able to live and succeed in the culture immigrants from the old world had established in the new world. Some schools that had been operated earlier as mission schools may have received a small federal government allowance on entering this program. Coqualeetza, the school Frank attended, was one of these.

In 1884 Coqualeetza was founded as a day school. The founders were Methodist missionaries, Charles and Caroline Tate, and they did so at their own expense. Two years later they began receiving money from the Methodist Woman's Missionary Society and built a residential school, but unfortunately in 1891 it burnt down. At that time the school received some help from the federal government to help rebuild it. Slowly it expanded, and by the time Frank attended in 1924 it hosted two large dormitories as part of the school.[3]

Many First Nation parents were opposed to such schooling and devastated by the resulting long months of separation from their children. Some hid their offspring, but if or when priests or law officers found them they were forcibly wrested from parents and taken off to school. Compulsory attendance at residential schools did not end until 1948 after the 1947 report of a Special Joint Committee resulted in a subsequent amendment of the Indian Act.[4] In reality, however, the only parents to whom the change gave choice were those on reserves large enough to warrant the cost of establishing a school there. Then native children like all those who attended public schools in the rest of the province returned home when the school day was over. When a reserve had its own school the band was given a choice of the religious denomination of the teacher to be employed and could choose depending on the Christian belief of the majority of parents.[5] For those living in remote regions, there was only compulsory residential schooling. For them choice was impossible because attendance in school was mandatory for everyone, and a public school was too distant from home.

Residential schooling remains controversial to this day. There have been numerous reports of abuse: physical, mental and sexual. In all, approximately eighty thousand First Nations children attended these schools from 1928 until the last school closed in 1996.[6]

Unlike many First Nations parents, Frank's parents (both by birth and by adoption) believed it was in their children's best interests, and in the interests of the Nisga'a Nation, for them to be educated. They chose Coqualeetza, the Methodist Mission School located in Sardis (now part of Chilliwack) in the Lower Mainland of British Columbia, because it was recommended by the Anglican missionaries in Kincolith and Greenville. Four years after Frank first attended Coqualeetza, it evolved into a government-funded residential school. Little changed. Funding came from the federal government but the curriculum and staff remained the same.

In late August of 1924, Frank impatiently awaited the arrival of the steamer that would transport him down the coast to school.[7] Because it was farthest north, Nass Harbour was the first port from which the *Cardena* would collect pupils. On board was Mr. G.H. Raley, the principal of Coqualeetza. His duty was to shepherd the students on their journey south. Never before had Frank left Nisga'a territory or travelled on a ship, bus or train. In later life he told his wife that it was with great excitement that he looked forward to the trip.

Along with his older brother Henry Clark, Frank said his goodbyes, and with an eager step and eyes agog, but perhaps with a twinge of anxiety at leaving all he had ever known behind, he walked up the gangplank of the ship. He had just turned nine years old earlier that month, on August 3. Two years later their younger brother Phillip would join them.

Once on board, Frank explored the new Union Steamship *Cardena* on which he would be living for four days and nights.[8] The *Cardena* had varying accommodations for passengers consisting of two suites, forty-two cabins, 132 berths and sixty bunks. The students occupied the cheapest accommodation. The ship, however, had comfortable main lounges and dining saloons that were open to all passengers.

Once the crew had cast off and the whistle sounded, the ship was on its way to the next stop at Kitimat. As the steamship sailed down the coast, it would stop at every cannery (Hartley Bay, Ocean Falls, Prince Rupert and others) to pick up both tinned and fresh salmon because the ship had a large refrigerated compartment.[9] In addition, pupils from other First Nations were taken on board. At canneries where there was no dock, a scow was used for landing. With keen interest Frank and the other children watched this process from the ship. Students were not allowed to go ashore, even though at times it took many hours to load the cargo.

Once they arrived in Vancouver, an interurban tram, a cross between a train and a streetcar, took the students to Chilliwack and then a few kilometres south to Sardis where the tracks made a circle near the school. Within minutes, the tram disappeared on its return run to Vancouver. Frank later told his brother Phillip that, as he stood with his few belongings at his side and stared at the imposing structure, he felt strange and lonely. In all, the school housed some two hundred boys and two hundred girls in separate dormitories.[10]

Only English was spoken in the school, and for many students this was a problem, but Frank and his siblings had learned enough at home to understand it fairly well. All four parents spoke English, and previously Frank had attended the mission school in Greenville where English was used, as well as learning it from his parents and his playmates, the Donaldson children.

English was the language used in all schools for First Nations because each nation spoke a different language, and there was a need for a common language of instruction. As well, English was necessary for communication outside reserves, so it was considered a necessary skill by the authorities who ran the schools. In some cases, no doubt, there was an animus against the native languages.

The language barrier, new customs and different expectations made life difficult for many students. Some schools imposed the punishment of having a student's mouth washed out with soap if he or she spoke their native language. The children were sometimes very young — the residential schools took children between the ages of six and fifteen. Students were away from home and family for the first time and were transported to a completely different environment from the one they had always known. Facing a situation like the one that was forced upon many First Nations children would be difficult for any child.

Frank was determined to make the best of his new life. He understood well the purpose for which he had been sent. Initially, life at the school was not easy because he was small for his age and in his first year was often picked on by the older boys. There was a nickname waiting for him in his dormitory. His older brother Henry had been given the name of "Sweet" by his classmates because of his love of chocolate and candy. Immediately, his roommates proclaimed that Frank would be known as "Young Sweet," and when Phillip arrived two years later Frank graduated to "Middle Sweet."

Although bullied in the beginning, Frank had a winning personality and soon made many friends. His popularity with the other students increased when he became "the Messenger." The girls' dormitory was separated from the boys', and some of the older boys wanted to pass love notes to their favourite girls. Frank could run fast and was good at devising ways of not being caught, and so was very successful in delivering notes and letters. Frank was eventually elected class representative.[11]

The curriculum at the school consisted of two parts: the morning was devoted to academic studies and the afternoons to more practical pursuits, some of which helped lower the cost of running the school. Students were taught simple tasks, such as how to make a bed; Frank won a prize for his. They learned how to plant a garden and were assigned chores that needed to be done around the school. Frank milked cows every morning before classes and then made butter. He was proud that he could get more milk from a cow than anyone else. In addition to success in these jobs he was a good student academically.

Sports were an important part of the curriculum. Dr. R.C. Scott from the nearby United Church, along with Mr. Peck, who taught English at Coqualeetza, coached soccer, or "football" as it was called at the school. As well as coaching, Dr. Scott and Mr. Peck would sometimes play the game along with the boys. Frank, who was a good runner, turned out to be an excellent player and was given the position of centre forward. After their early morning practices the team was treated to bacon and eggs for breakfast as a reward for their hard work. This made the sport popular,

Sketch of Coqualeetza Residential School, Sardis, BC. Courtesy of Leith Harper, from a 1931 badly faded photo of the school supplied by Frank Lindley.

and everyone wanted to join the team. The team turned out to be very strong. In 1935 and again in 1936 they played against the Sardis Stars for the Chilliwack Valley Championship and won.[12]

There was an unfortunate incident during an unusually cold winter in the Fraser Valley. Frank was on the senior soccer team playing against the school's intermediate team, of which Phillip was a member. Frank slipped on a frozen puddle and broke his arm. It never healed properly, and ever after his shoulder would sometimes pop out. For this reason, he was rejected when later in life he volunteered to serve in the army during the Second World War.

Later that same year, during a baseball game, Frank attempted to catch a ball without using a glove and broke a finger. For the rest of his life his little finger would never bend forward and would cross over his middle finger when he used a pen or pencil. Regardless of these mishaps he continued to play, and neither injury prevented him from participating in a very full sports program.[13]

One day a bicycle arrived at the school for Frank. It was a surprise present from his adoptive father, Chief Arthur Calder. Everyone at school wanted rides on it, so Frank charged for them, and his friends were convinced he made more money than the teachers. This may have been true, for the teachers were poorly paid, and at least once Phillip remembers that a teacher borrowed money from his brother. Frank used his money to go to movies and sometimes paid for friends to go with him. In later life he told his wife, Tamaki, that he remembered during the "love scenes" they would deliberately crack peanut shells as loudly as they could.

Saturdays were time off, and Phillip recalls sitting idly outside the school fences, with Frank and his friends, watching the hop-pickers collect the hops that grew in abundance in the fields outside Chilliwack. The pickers had large boxes to fill and worked in the hot sun for the pittance of four dollars a box.[14]

During his school years, Frank returned to the Nass Valley for two months every summer to fish. Instead of fishing with his father, who used a powerboat, he chose to fish with his brother-in-law, Walter Calder, on his sailboat. He liked the quiet. He began gill netting when he was twelve years old and continued to do so through all his years of schooling.

Not all students chose to return home for the long holiday. Phillip tells of two summers when he lived at school but spent much time in White Rock. He loved its wide sand beaches and long pier. Failure to return home was often a contentious issue with parents, who felt they were losing connection with their children. There are accounts that even when children did return home they would criticize the traditional ways in which their parents had brought them up. The longer children were away, the greater became the feeling of rejection on the part of parents.

Unlike many students at residential schools, Frank always said that his memories of school were good ones. Years later Frank told his wife: "Mr. Birie used the strap for discipline just as it was used in all schools in British Columbia at that time but in our school there was never any abuse. I was never strapped. When I first came, it was because I was small for my age, and Dr. Raley wouldn't allow small boys to be strapped even if they did misbehave. There were good schools and bad schools. I was lucky and was sent to a good one."

Residential schooling only went as far as grade 10, but Frank decided that he wanted to attend a public high school and obtain a high school graduation certificate. His parents considered this an admirable goal, and arrangements were made for him to enrol at Chilliwack High School. He continued living at Coqualeetza while attending, and every day rode his bike four miles into Chilliwack. He was the only Aboriginal student in the school. In order to succeed at Chilliwack High, Frank had to learn a higher level of English than what had been demanded at Coqualeetza. In fact, he put in long hours studying and using the language. During his later years in politics, he was often heard to say, "What I learned of the English language at Chilliwack High enabled me to read law books later in life." In 1937, after residing primarily at Coqualeetza for twelve years, Frank graduated from high school.

During his career, and after his name began to be noticed in newspapers, teachers and fellow students from Chilliwack High would be asked about him. They described him as being quiet, reserved and outstanding in athletics, a soccer and track star, who also played lacrosse. Frank spoke far less of the years at Chilliwack High than of those at Coqualeetza, perhaps because they were more difficult for him. It is never easy being first and he was one of the first Aboriginal students in Canada to attend a public high school. He graduated with good final grades.

During Frank's years at school he matured into a full-grown man. He was short, which was noticeable in almost every group photograph but strong and sturdy with a lean athletic build. He had a broad forehead, black hair, deep brown eyes and a serious expression. As a young man he was considered good looking and by some even handsome.

The summer after he graduated, Frank returned to the Nass to fish — as he had done in previous years. One day, when he was relaxing at home in the Clark house in Mill Bay and listening to "The Bells of St. Mary's" on the record player, a messenger arrived from Greenville with devastating news. His adoptive father, Arthur Calder, had died suddenly. It saddened Frank and many good memories flooded back of the man who had brought him up as his own son. They had shared many experiences, and he had received much important guidance from his chieftain father over the years. His passing would leave a huge gap in his life. He knew his mother, Louisa, would be devastated and would want him close by. He immediately left for home. In Greenville a traditional Nisga'a ceremony was planned as well as a Christian funeral to honour Chief Na-qua-oon's memory. Hundreds of Nisga'a throughout the Nass attended. The position of new chief now passed to Frank's birth father, Job Clark.

For Frank, a period of mourning followed during which he engaged in much thought and made a decision about his future. When First Nations students left residential school, they usually went back to their reserve or tried to get a job in a city. City jobs were hard for them to find because prejudice was rampant among the general population. Frank attempted neither. A year after being the first Aboriginal student to graduate from a public high school, he enrolled at the University of British Columbia and became the first Canadian Status Indian to attend university. Frank chose the affiliated Anglican Theological College.[15] The college had opened in 1929 and provided residence for its students. At the time, Frank believed the ministry was the only profession that would make him equal to the white man. As he grew older and more experienced, he was heard to remark, "I wish I had taken law instead."

As a student, Frank took an active part in university life. He played for the varsity soccer team and was one of their notable players. He was mentioned several times in the campus newspaper.[16] Like many students, he was forced to work to stay solvent, and every summer — and sometimes for longer periods — he returned home to make money in the fishing industry. It was the only way he could pay his tuition, so it took him two years longer than the usual four years to graduate. Even so, his classmates of 1943 insisted that he be part of their graduation group photograph. During the months when university was in session, he worked as a barber on weekends cutting the hair of his fellow students. Throughout his years of education, he did not receive any scholarships, bursaries, educational grants, student loans or subsidies of any kind. Financial support for students in higher education was very scarce at that time.

In 1943 while still a student at UBC, Frank gave a speech at the fourteenth Annual Convention of the Native Brotherhood and Native Sisterhood of British Columbia at Cape Mudge on Quadra Island across from Campbell River. His topic was "The Legal Status of American and Canadian Indians."[17] A year later in 1944, he became president of the North American Indian Brotherhood. Through his work with these organizations Frank's awareness of the lack of recognition for First Nations rights increased. He was determined after graduation to work for equality for his people.

Frank graduated in 1945, becoming the first Aboriginal in Canada to graduate from a university. He wanted to continue with higher education and planned to enrol at the University of Washington State and take his doctorate in theology. This would be expensive, and he knew he would have to save as much money as possible beforehand.

For three years he worked at the Edmunds Walker fish plant in Prince Rupert. He joined the United Fishermen and Allied Workers Union and held membership card no. 5961 from 1943 to 1955. During his time there, he became an elected union representative and secretary of the Brotherhood. His long-term plan was to become involved in social service and work among the First Nations of British Columbia. His life, however, never followed the plan he had designed. Fate intervened.

CHAPTER 3

The First Elections,
1949–1953

IN LATE APRIL 1949, Frank was taking a few days off as tallyman from
the fish cannery in Prince Rupert before the height of the fishing season
began. He was spending them at home with the Clark family in Nass
Harbour. Unexpectedly, this short holiday proved to be a crossroads in
his life. The direction he had planned for his future changed dramatically from one dedicated to the church and social service to one in politics.

Provincial politics in British Columbia in the 1940s were different
from what they are today. Then there were two major political parties at
the federal level, the Liberals and the Conservatives. In 1941, in BC, they
had joined forces to form a coalition government.[1] Together they attained a majority; it was the only way they could defeat the Cooperative
Commonwealth Federation Party (CCF), which was very strong in BC
and a forerunner of today's New Democratic Party. In BC, throughout
the forties, the Liberals had more seats than the Conservatives but, by
themselves, they had not enough to prevent the CCF from forming a
minority government. So even though they were arch-enemies federally,

provincially the Liberals and Conservatives were united out of necessity.

Not surprisingly, the coalition government had internal problems and was not overly popular with the people. However, traditional voters of both the Liberal and Conservative parties considered a marriage of convenience a better choice than allowing the socialist CCF party to form the government. Nonetheless, coalition support slowly continued to wane.

At that time, no Canadian province had granted the right to vote to people of Chinese, East Indian or Japanese descent. The same restriction applied to Aboriginal people. Early in 1949 under the coalition government, British Columbia became the first province in Canada to rescind this racist voting law and allowed ethnic minorities to vote in the province. (Federally, the Chinese were allowed the vote in 1947.)[2] It took an additional eleven years until 1960, before native peoples gained the right to vote in federal elections.[3]

In 1949, the coalition government of British Columbia called an election for June 15, the first in which First Nations people could vote. Few voters in the province believed the new votes would make a difference in the final results. The riding of Atlin, in which the Nass River was located, would prove to be an exception. The northern riding encompassed the Nisga'a homeland.

That spring the Reverend W.D. Smith, a Liberal and the sitting coalition member for the riding, began his campaign in the riding of Atlin. When he arrived by Union steamship at Nass Harbor, however, the sky closed in, the wind whipped up and a major storm ensued. Mr. Smith was stranded, and the Clark family who were working at the cannery took him in. He lived at their house for three days until the weather cleared. At night, talk around the fireplace inevitably turned to politics.

One evening, as everyone was relaxing after dinner, Frank asked the visitor, "Who is running against you?"

"No one," came the prompt reply.

There was silence for a while, and then Phillip frowned and looked at his brother. "Why don't you run?"

"I haven't any money. For a campaign a lot is needed. I couldn't." Frank shook his head.

Mr. Smith looked thoughtful. "I think you could. The native population would finance you. It would be a big step forward for them to have their own candidate."

Later that night Frank made the decision to launch his political career. Mr. Smith had an extra set of nomination papers, which he gave to him. The next day, Frank's mother, Emily, phoned Victoria to find out the exact procedure that Frank had to follow to file them. He began by joining the CCF party and became their candidate for Atlin. Jack Scott, who had run for them in former years, had not sought the Atlin nomination again. Frank was proud to represent the CCF party — for sixteen years their members had worked hard for the right of minorities to vote and had been instrumental in the right finally being granted to Aboriginals. Mr. Smith had been correct when he said the native people would support Frank. The Nisga'a and other First Nations people all contributed and helped raise enough money so that he could open a campaign office in Stewart.

The election was hard-fought, but throughout the entire eight weeks Mr. Smith was confident of winning. Even though he thought it was good for the First Nations to have a candidate of their own, he did not think a thirty-four-year-old opponent with almost no political experience had a chance. He forgot to take into consideration that earlier that year in Bella Coola Frank had been elected secretary of the Native Brotherhood of British Columbia, and in addition was an elected representative of the United Fishermen and Allied Workers Union. These people supported him and liked the platform on which he was running: "equal rights for all."

The result was close. On the night of the election Mr. Smith was declared winner by 307 votes to Frank's 191, but a large number of Aboriginal voters in the ridings of Port Edward and Carlisle had cast ballots in an advance poll before leaving to fish. When these were counted the next day, the vote was reversed, and it was announced that Frank had won by six votes: 376 to 370.[4] He spent the day after his election working a fourteen-hour shift at the cannery in Prince Rupert.[5] To his co-workers all he kept saying was, "I'm still surprised." Mr. Smith put in a request for a judicial recount but after reviewing the vote withdrew it.

Frank took his seat in the Legislative Assembly of British Columbia as a member of the Opposition; the coalition had won again. He was the youngest member of the legislature but not by much. It was a toss-up between Frank and J.D. McRae of Prince Rupert. Frank was the younger by a few months although both were thirty-four.

The most colourful legislative opening ever witnessed by the public followed the swearing in ritual for elected members of the twenty-second assembly. Fourteen minutes before three in the afternoon, fifteen twenty-five-pound field guns echoed across Victoria's inner harbour to mark the opening. Chief William Scow, president of the Native Brotherhood of BC and Chief Frank Assu, president of the Native Brotherhood of Indians, attended in colourful full regalia. Chief Scow was draped in a button blanket and Chief Assu in the ceremonial robes of his forefathers. Both wore elaborate headdresses as they presented Premier Byron Johnson with a document thanking the legislature for giving Indians the vote and reaffirming their pledge of allegiance and loyalty to the Crown.

from **FRANK CALDER**
CCF CANDIDATE

• THE FIRST •
NATIVE INDIAN
CANDIDATE
IN CANADA

Frank as pictured on his first campaign flyer, 1949.

It was a day of many firsts. It was the first time that people belonging to minorities had voted for anyone who governed them. It was the first time a Status Indian had become an elected member of any Canadian government. It was also the first time a Speaker of a Canadian-elected legislative body was a woman. Nancy Hodges, the MLA from Victoria, was not only the first female Speaker of an elected body in Canada, but the first woman to hold such a position in the entire British Commonwealth of Nations. Naturally, both she and Frank received a great deal of media attention.[6] Frank was overheard to say to her, "You and I, Madame Speaker, have made a bit of a noise today and just between ourselves now, it's a somewhat pleasant feeling isn't it?"[7] She smiled back at him.

Traditionally, a short time after the swearing in of a new legislative session a formal ball at Government House was held to celebrate the event. This year the Lieutenant Governor, the Honourable Charles Banks, and his wife hosted it. It was a gala affair with speeches, dancing and an elaborate buffet. Drinks were served. There was much speculation and whispering behind closed doors as to what would happen if Frank attended. It was illegal to serve alcohol to any First Nations person and it was illegal for one of them to accept an alcoholic drink. Many in the crowd were watching surreptitiously. The waiter passed the tray, offered one to Frank, he accepted, and that was the end of the matter. It would have been an interesting eventuality to have had the Lieutenant Governor charged with an offence for having served alcohol to an Aboriginal person, or for an elected member of the legislature to be charged for accepting one.

A few months later in February, Frank gave his maiden speech. He stood and began by saying, "I have heard so many members going to bat for the poor Indian (now that they have the vote) that I think I should go to bat for the white man," and received much laughter from the house. He proceeded by recalling how, "One hundred and fifty years ago, when the white man started trading along the coast he adopted a Chinookan language in which to communicate with the Indians. Now through the process of time the Chinookan tongue has all but disappeared but today I can return the compliment and speak to you in English." Again there was much laughter.

Soon his speech turned serious when he said, "The vote, however, has paved the way for new rights and new responsibilities. Indians now have a legal voice in the affairs of the province and a right to ask for equality of citizenship. Today the Indian stands as a second-class citizen, robbed even of his native rights, his water, fish and timber rights, half his traplines are gone. . . . My picture of a full Magna Carta for natives is equality of opportunity in education, in health, in employment and in citizenship." He called upon the legislature to establish a Bill of Rights for British Columbia that would enshrine such rights in law. He sat down to a roar of applause.[8] The little boy that so long ago had been predicted to "move that mountain" had started on the long road for which he was destined.

CCF Newsletter in Augumn 1949, after Frank's election.

Frank began the process of learning his way around the convoluted systems of the political scene, all the while considering the best ways to further the rights of his people. By "his people" he meant everyone in the riding of Atlin and throughout BC. He was heard on many occasions — when it was assumed that he represented only First Nations — to emphasize, "I represent *all* the people in the riding of Atlin." He was hard working and soon became a member of three standing committees: Standing Orders and Private Bills, Municipal Matters and Social Welfare and Education.[9]

In late March, not long after his maiden speech, he introduced a motion asking the house to pass a Bill of Rights, for all people of the province. In it he included the following:

> – Freedom of religion;
> – Free expression;
> – Freedom from arbitrary imprisonment;
> – Equal opportunity in employment;
> – Engagement in all occupations;
> – Ownership and occupation of property;
> – Membership in professional and trade associations;
> – Education.[10]

Frank knew that in many respects such rights did not extend to all the ethnic minorities; he wanted a declaration of human rights passed that would stand as a marker against which action could be taken when or if rights were denied.

The attorney general, Gordon Wisner, refused resolution for the bill on the grounds that the proposed Bill of Rights was unnecessary. He believed such rights were already granted because, in his view, they were embodied in Common Law — even though at this time minorities were restricted from full citizenship. Those against the bill rationalized their belief on the basis that minorities were adequately cared for under Canadian law, and Aboriginals were specifically cared for through reserves, schooling, medical care and treaty payments. Therefore, they considered it fair that these people were ineligible for any of the following benefits:

– Old age pensions;
– Social welfare payments;
– Ownership of land;
– Grants of homestead land;
– The right to purchase or consume alcohol;
– Voting in federal elections.

A written reply to Wisner's refusal came from Mr. Darwin Charlton of the Vancouver Labour Council: "British Columbia's laws allow discrimination in restrictive covenants, services given by hotels and resorts and in the hiring of personnel. It is an empty boast for Mr. Wisner to say these rights of individual freedom are embodied in Common Law."[11]

In July 1951 the government in Ottawa passed a revised federal Indian Act. It was a disappointment to the Native Brotherhood of British Columbia, because, despite previously submitted requests to transfer control over most Aboriginal issues to the province, they remained in the hands of the federal government. They had requested the transfer in the belief that at the provincial level their problems would have a better chance of being addressed. Few transfers were dealt with but there was one important exception: the revised act transferred liquor law to the provinces. Immediately, Frank took up the cause of liquor rights, not only because he knew it was the source of many inequities, but because it was one right that the BC legislature now had the power to change. Liquor privileges had long been a thorny issue on all First Nations reserves.

Prohibition during the 1920s in the United States had led to a great deal of illegal activity, and prohibition had exactly the same result when it was imposed on Aboriginal people in BC. Law enforcement agencies lacked the resources to prevent liquor from reaching Aboriginals. Moreover, when it arrived on reserves it did so at sharply inflated prices and was often of very suspicious quality. At times, it led to sickness and occasionally to poisoning. Distilled moonshine, with all the dangers of inept, amateur production, was made by both First Nations people and white men and sold illegally to others. It was usually very potent, hence the term "firewater." There was also rank discrimination in the treatment of drunken Aboriginals compared to white people. A drunken white person would be sent home to sober up or be given a fine depending on behaviour, but Aboriginals would face a fine and a criminal charge.

Bizarre situations driven by avarice and profit occurred, and police action was sporadic and often unavailable. In Greenville, the following incident was included in a missionary's diary and demonstrates the greed and exploitation that evolved from the prohibition of the sale of alcohol:

> In the fall after the fishing season was over a two mast schooner anchored in front of the village. It was loaded with whiskey and sold not in bottles but in four-gallon tins before anyone in Greenville reported it. The next day four RCMP constables arrested the white sellers and confiscated their boat along with the remaining whiskey but not before most of it had been sold at exorbitant prices. Needless to say the spree that followed led to fights, sex and rude laughter none of which was usual.[12]

This incident was reported and the sellers punished but most such cases were overlooked.

It was a long uphill battle to get the province to approve changes to the existing law, but Frank was determined. As an Opposition member, he did not have the ear of the government but nevertheless introduced a private member's bill on liquor reform. It was voted down by the coalition. It was not until the next legislature, under the Social Credit government that Frank gained any support for the issue, and then it was only a partial victory. In the later part of 1952, Aboriginals were given the legal right to consume beer and liquor in licensed public places, though they were still prohibited from buying it for consumption at home.

The passage of the new liquor law for Aboriginals did not come without recriminations from some members of the legislature. There was drunkenness and disorderly conduct, especially in rural outlets near reserves. Several MLAs, especially those from the Fraser Valley, rose in the house and, citing abuse, asked that liquor rights for Aboriginals be rescinded.

Frank replied to these charges, "I don't think you are proud of your skid rows either. The white man introduced alcohol to the Indians and now he has to teach him how to drink."[13]

At about this time, Frank faced an even more difficult issue. His party, the CCF, supported returning fishing rights to former Japanese fishers from whom they had been confiscated after the attack on Pearl Harbor in 1942. However, most of the rights had been taken over by First Nations people. This placed Frank in a complicated position. The Japanese had been unfairly treated, but his constituents were angry over the prospect of losing fishing rights they believed they had owned since 1942. As well, before the Japanese arrived, First Nations people had fished the waters exclusively. The herring fishery was especially important to them. Naturally they expected Frank's support.

After much thought, Calder suggested that a committee be formed of both Japanese and Aboriginal people to settle the issue. In June of 1951, Frank was elected chairman of the committee. Under his guidance, the matter was settled by convincing the Japanese to become members of the United Fishermen and Allied Workers Union — as First Nations fishers had done previously. The resolution created harmony because both sides were united under a single body and through it could work together for benefits for all fishers.[14] Both sides agreed that there was enough fish for all, and that, through common membership, both parties would have equal means to air future grievances.

The next year Frank fought for an important benefit for fishers: Workman's Compensation. The legislation passed, but with an amendment declaring that the fishers, rather than the canneries and fleet owners, would pay the insurance premiums. In many industries it was the owners and company that paid at least part of the premiums. Even though he was disappointed, Frank voted in favour because at least it offered some protection for unemployment caused by accidents. The new legislation received an overwhelming response from fishers, and they poured into Victoria to register. Frank was on hand to greet them.[15]

In the autumn of the same year their Royal Highnesses, Princess Elizabeth and Prince Philip, toured Canada. Victoria was one of their stops. It was a great occasion and all members of the legislature were invited to a special luncheon in honour of the visiting royalty, held at the Empress Hotel. Frank was delighted to be included and especially to be singled out by Prince Philip as one of the guests to whom he and the Princess spoke a few words. In his first scrapbook, he preserved both his invitation and the menu of the sumptuous luncheon.[16]

Meanwhile, the problems of the coalition government were becoming increasingly obvious. In January of 1952, a split in the party occurred and it became apparent that an election could not be far off. The house dissolved into quibbling and name-calling, each party attempting to discredit the other. An article written in the *Vancouver News Herald* at that time praised Frank as one member who did not participate in petty name-calling and kept to his agenda. To serve as a diversion for the house, Frank rose to speak and startled everyone by doing so in the Nisga'a tongue. He continued for a full three minutes and ended his oration by saying, "and now for the benefit of those of you who are newcomers to our country I will interpret in English."[17] Laughter resulted and it lightened the mood.

An election was called for July 12, 1952. Frank returned to campaign in Atlin. As the major opposition party, the CCF had high hopes of forming a majority government, but the political landscape was changing. A new party, Social Credit, under WAC Bennett, was running candidates in most ridings. Many people believed they were nothing but a fringe party, but a surprise was in store.

This time on voting day there was no doubt about the outcome in Atlin and no need to wait for absentee votes. The final count showed Frank had defeated Mr. Smith by a wide margin. However, his party, the CCF, faced a great disappointment. It had elected one member fewer than the new Social Credit party, so the Socreds and not the CCF formed a government. It was a narrow, unforeseen upset, eighteen members to nineteen. WAC Bennett became premier, but it was of a minority government. Running a minority government is difficult for any political party and, like most, Bennett's was destined to be short lived. In spite of steps to improve infrastructure, especially highways, the first Socred government was defeated in a non-confidence vote for education financing on March 24, 1953.

Voters went to the polls again on June 9, 1953, and Frank faced his third election battle in four years. The CCF hoped the electorate was disenchanted enough with the new party that they would win. However, even though Frank was re-elected easily, his party was unquestionably defeated. The Social Credit party won a decisive majority of twenty-eight seats to the CCF's fourteen. The Liberals were left with four, and the Conservatives with only a single seat.

An interesting sideline to Calder's victory in Atlin was the amount of money spent by each of the three parties. Expenses for MacKay of the Conservatives totalled $4,000, W.D. Smith of the Liberals spent $1,938, and Calder of the CCF came in a distant third at $128. The candidate who had spent the least won. In all of Frank's election campaigns he never had large sums to spend on his campaigns.[18]

The second Social Credit victory marked the beginning of a new era in politics in British Columbia. Socred government majorities would continue until 1991 with the exception of three years from 1972 to 1975, when the New Democratic party (transformed from the CCF) formed the government.

CHAPTER 4

The Legislature,
1953–1956

THE MAJORITY SOCIAL CREDIT party had been founded in the neighbouring province of Alberta by William Aberhart. It was a strong political force there and, with the favourable vote for the Socreds in 1953, it became a strong force in British Columbia. In its original form the party believed that all tax money collected from the people should be returned to them in one form or another, either through credits or cash payments, if the treasury warranted it. As a result, it was sometimes ridiculed as the "funny money" party, but in spite of that, it was destined to dominate British Columbia politics for some forty years.

The new government was sworn into office with high expectations for change by the voters. Calder, along with his fellow CCF members, was disappointed with the election results. The CCF had spent years fighting the Liberals, the Conservatives and the coalition and just when it seemed the CCF was on the verge of a breakthrough along had come this brand new party that had snatched their dreams of power away. Those who believed in CCF policies felt it was a defeat for the poor and the working classes. This sentiment, however, was not shared by most people in the province. The collective hope seemed to be that the new party would be a "breath of fresh air" after years of coalition infighting. In the past, major urban centres in the south had always dominated provincial governments. It was a pleasant surprise to many that the new leader, WAC Bennett, was from Kelowna, at that time only a small town on Okanagan Lake.

Mr. Bennett was a character larger than life, a hard-working hardware merchant and a teetotaler with a strong Protestant work ethic. Inevitably, with the initials WAC, "ky" was added and he was sometimes fondly, and sometimes not so fondly, referred to as "Wacky Bennett." He would prove to be an extremely astute politician.

The new government did not disappoint voters, and change began to take place. There had even been some speculation that the new premier might appoint Frank to a cabinet post. During the Socred's election campaign Mr. Bennett had been heard to say that he felt the Indians should have representation in the government and that in his opinion Frank Calder was not a true member of the CCF. In spite of rumours, in the end Frank did not receive an appointment, and he denied that one had ever been discussed with him.

Two changes that Calder had long pressed for, however, and that were significant for First Nations people, took place fairly rapidly. In 1953 attendance in all public schools in British Columbia was made accessible to First Nations children.[1] Immediately, Frank made an open plea for parents to take advantage of this opportunity.

The second change quickly followed. Robert Sommers, the Minister of Lands and Forests, introduced Bill 48 that gave First Nations people the right to own land outside reserves. At one time natives did have this right but when the colony of British Columbia joined the Confederation of Canada it ceased to exist. Several years before the Socreds introduced the bill, a newspaperman Mr. Archie Flucke (and Mr. Bruce McKelvie, a provincial historian), had unearthed a letter written by former governor Douglas in 1874 to Dr. I. W. Powell, Commissioner, stating the colony's ongoing policy for dealing with native lands. The policy stated, "Natives whether on reserves or not, have the same rights as any other British subject of acquiring lands by purchase or pre-emption."[2]

When BC entered Confederation, the Indians were promised just as generous treatment as they had received from the colonial government, but somehow and somewhere this privilege was removed from the Act of Union. At last, the right was restored. Frank had promoted the two changes in every speech he had made on equal rights. They had all included education and land ownership.

The new era ushered in by the Social Credit government was one of prosperity. Phil Gaglardi, who had been appointed Minister of Highways, was responsible for a very noticeable improvement that helped both the economy and the government's image. He began building new, high-quality highways throughout the interior of the province. Calder supported his policy of highway construction and spoke of the need for roads to isolated places in his riding. Vast areas that had formerly been reachable only by ill-kept gravel roads were gradually becoming readily accessible. A humorous incident regarding Mr. Gaglardi and his road building has long been remembered. At one point in his career near his hometown of Kamloops, "Flying Phil," as he was sometimes dubbed, was stopped for speeding by the RCMP. He explained to the officer that he was minister of highways and explained that he "was only testing the curves."

Frank championed many problems that existed throughout the north and that were severely affecting everyone in his huge, remote riding. He had spoken of the need to build roads, but he also addressed unequal treatment for Aboriginals in such issues as old age pensions, forestry rights, trapping rights and fishing rights. He believed equality should be enshrined in law. In one speech he asked the government to find a method by which Indians could obtain fire insurance. It wasn't available on reserves.

While Frank was fighting for the rights of people whose roots to the land went back hundreds and hundreds of years and which were largely ignored by the media, a radical group called the Sons of Freedom was grabbing headlines almost daily. They were a radical splinter sect of the Doukhobors who, because of religious persecution, had left Russia in the late 1800s. They had been led to Canada by the lordly Peter Verigin and had settled in northeast Saskatchewan. They believed all property and living should be communal, and they refused to recognize government authority. They were excellent farmers, however, did well with their land, and became prosperous. As time progressed their original communes broke up and many farmers chose to own their land independently. This caused a break in the sect, and Verigin led the more orthodox members to a new home in the Kootenay region of BC. He died in 1925 in a suspicious train explosion that to this day remains a mystery.[3] After Verigin's death the sons of Freedom had slowly become increasingly radical, setting fire to property and using violence to support their beliefs.

Calder rose in the house and spoke on the issue. He noted the preponderance of attention the Sons of Freedom were receiving in the legislature, and said, "These people are relative newcomers. . . . You are very fortunate we [First Nations] do not burn down schools and blow up bridges [as they do]." He stressed his point by saying, "Perhaps if we used the same tactics we would get more action. Scrap the Indian Affairs Advisory Committee. It has become a big joke. Indians' problems should be discussed here on the floor of this house, not in some building down the street. If labour has any problem it goes to the [House] Labour Committee ... if agriculture has any problems they take them to the [House] Agricultural Committee. I say scrap Indian Affairs because it has done nothing. Bring the problems of the Indians where they belong . . . to their elected representatives."[4] Frank believed it was entirely unfair that disruptive radicals were given so much time and resources while the problems of Aboriginals were often dismissed on technicalities.

The mayhem the Sons of Freedom were creating did not lessen. Their beliefs included shunning clothing and refusing to send their children to school. When they thought that any of their beliefs were challenged, they retaliated. When truant officers forced their sons and daughters to school, they burned down the school. There was a saying at the time, "It's easy to know when you are in Kootenay country because the schools are always new." Other forms of protest included blowing up bridges and women parading naked in public places, including outside the courthouse in Vancouver.

The problems they created were serious and were frequently discussed on the floor of the house where Frank argued the problems of First Nations people should be raised. A specific incident occurred that he believed illustrated the disproportionate time and resources allotted to this group in comparison to that granted First Nations people. Randolph Harding, the member for the Kootenays, stood in the house and asked that an official visit be paid to his riding in order to assure municipal officials that the government was doing everything possible to stop further outbreaks of arson and bombings. Frank believed it illustrated his point because the house took Harding's request seriously. They agreed to the visit. No such request had ever been granted to resolve any First Nation problems.

The violence finally stopped when the children of the Sons of Freedom were taken from their parents and placed in residential schools modelled after those First Nations children attended. This action appeared to give sobering second thoughts to many of the radicals, and most became reconciled to the mores of Canadian society. Those who would not accept restrictions of any kind formed a splinter group and emigrated to South America. Little was ever heard from them thereafter.

The next October Frank stood in the house and urged that an Indian be appointed to the Senate.[5] The policy of his party, the CCF, was that the Senate should be abolished. His party did not approve of Canada having a Senate, appointed or not, and wanted Canada's senior legislative body eliminated. However, Frank's position differed. He believed that if there was going to be a Senate in existence in Canada an Aboriginal should be a member of it. It was the first and would not be the last time Frank would place his personal and moral beliefs against those of his own party.

Calder's goal of having an Aboriginal appointed as a senator was not achieved until seven years later when John Diefenbaker, leader of the Progressive Conservative Party, became Canada's prime minister. He agreed with Frank's opinion and a few months after taking office in 1958 appointed James Gladstone of the Blackfoot Nation in Alberta a senator. Frank made a point of meeting with the new senator and having the Native Brotherhood of BC declare Gladstone an honorary member of the organization.[6]

Over the next three and a half years Calder became known as a tireless champion for First Nation people and, indeed, all northern residents. Issues such as roads and ambulance services affected everyone in his riding. In the legislature, time and again he brought in resolutions calling for medical services to be of the same quality in the north as those enjoyed by residents in the south. He emphasized the scarce northern supply of medical aid and the serious lack of doctors and nurses. He believed a mobile dental clinic should be established and that doctors, public health nurses and dentists should be headquartered in Stewart and from there visit outlying areas.

A specific issue he put forward in this session was a request to remove Indian Agent R.H. Sampson from his position.[7] Calder had received many complaints about Sampson, and some Aboriginals claimed that at times Sampson was unavailable to see anyone. Often, his only excuse was that he was too busy. For the Nisga'a and other First Nations people, it was no trivial event to travel all the way down the Nass to Prince Rupert, and they were not pleased to find that, after the long trip, they had to deal with Mr. Sampson's uncooperative, unfriendly attitude. The complaint was taken to Commissioner W.S. Arneil for resolution, and Sampson was replaced.

In March of 1954 a new provincial sales tax of five percent was imposed on goods and services to pay for universal medical coverage that had formerly been paid for through private insurance. Frank opposed it. He believed it squeezed natives to pay for others because, as he said, "We pay the five percent like everyone else but our reserves won't get a share of it [for hospitals] like municipalities do. Indians get medical and education services under the Indian Act and to cover their costs the province receives $300,000 annually from the federal government." In other words, Indians would be required to pay the new tax but the government of British Columbia would still collect $300,000 from the federal government for services to Indians. Frank termed it, "a low down dirty trick," and believed it was outright discrimination. He said, "Indians should be covered in the same way as all other residents through the new sales tax and should receive the same services as all others in the province."[8] He believed that, if Indians were going to pay the sales tax, the $300,000 from the federal government should be spent on upgrading other services on reserves. Mr. Martin, the minister in charge replied, "The matter will be studied," and subsequently the reserves did receive some additional benefits.

Free air ambulance service was sorely needed throughout the north. At that time critical cases were flown by plane or helicopter to Whitehorse, and even though medical care was covered, the patient or the community had to pay the cost of airfare. Such cost was prohibitive to many, and Frank suggested that a service be introduced patterned after the Northern Territory Medical Service in Australia. He argued that many lives had been lost for lack of such a service.

To further the cause, Frank arranged to meet for an informal discussion about air ambulance service with the president of Queen Charlotte Airlines. At the meeting Jim Spilsbury, president of the airline, told him that such an air ambulance service would require five planes and a helicopter based in each of five centres: Vancouver, Prince Rupert, Prince George, Ocean Falls and Kamloops.

The *CCF News* reported that the house sat silent as Frank rose to present the results of his investigation. He began by winding the "spell of the north," speaking of its vast area and resources that "staggered the imagination." He emphasized the dire need. The legislature seemed impressed but even though it was estimated at that time that an air ambulance service would cost some $200,000 per year, and hospital insurance reported a surplus of three million for the fiscal year, air ambulance service for the north was turned down. It took many years and an NDP government before such a service was established.[9] When the newspapers reported jeeringly that air ambulance service was Calder's pet topic because he had brought it up four times in four sessions of the legislature, Frank's response was that he would keep bringing it up until it was implemented.

The same month, Frank asked for a new provincial museum to be built, with the funding for it to be included in the next budget. He complained, "The present one is a disgrace; it's overcrowded and the Indian exhibits are jammed into the basement with the washrooms. That's not good enough.[10] The speaker of the house replied, "It certainly isn't." A new museum was taken up as a cause and the one that presently stands across from the legislature opened in August 1968. The museum's name was changed a year before it opened from the British Columbia Provincial Museum to the Royal British Columbia Museum to honour Queen Elizabeth II's visit when she toured Canada to commemorate Canada's 1967 centennial.

A poignant remembrance for Frank occurred at the celebration of the opening of the next legislative session in January 1956. He escorted Caroline Mack of Bella Coola to the formal ball at Government House. She was the first Aboriginal woman ever to attend such a function. The following description of her was given in the society pages of the *Vancouver Province* newspaper. She was, they said, "as lovely as those Indian maidens of Canadian song and verse ... but in modern dress, a bouffant, turquoise model clouding around her as she danced." Frank and his partner were widely photographed.[11]

A month later, the federal government amended the Indian Act and transferred to each province the authority to grant liquor rights to First Nations people. It meant that Frank could finally have the issue fully resolved. In the legislature he spoke against the present regulations that forbade Indians to enter liquor stores. "They can frequent beer parlors but are not allowed to take liquor home. It is based on the belief that Indians would go haywire if allowed in liquor stores. But Indians have been going haywire for years because they have been making their own stuff on their reserves." Frank further defended the change, saying, "One of the main reasons the legislature does not grant such rights is because it is loath to give up revenue in the form of fines that the Indians pay for violations. In Prince Rupert alone such fines total $20,000 per year and province wide they amount to $150,000."[12]

The provincial government was somewhat reluctant to make a change, so Frank developed a strategy that would force them to do so. He convinced the Nisga'a to hold a plebiscite on liquor rights on their reserve. Under the revised Indian Act it was their right to do so. The plebiscite passed and the next summer full liquor privileges were granted to the Nisga'a. It set a precedent. Now, any First Nation that held a similar successful plebiscite would obtain full liquor rights. The Nisga'a had led the way for equality for First Nations in one small respect under the law.

After the liquor bill had passed, the mayor of Prince Rupert (see appendix) congratulated Frank on its passage in a letter in which he said, "You handled this program masterfully and have accomplished something which nobody else in the Province had previously been able to do. Your strategy left the Attorney-General with no other choice but to accede to your request. The granting of equality in liquor rights is the first step towards equality in other fields." The law gave every reserve the right to decide for their nation (see appendix 2).

Immediately after the bill's passage, Calder wrote letters to the provincial attorney general, Robert Bonner, and the federal minister of justice, Davie Fulton. Frank knew that many abuses of alcohol would take place. His letters requested that, since liquor would now be allowed to Indians on reserves, the government should make provision for law and order. There were police enforcing order in the province's towns with liquor outlets, and he believed reserves should have the same kind of enforcement. He wrote, "We do not expect that authorities will place RCMP officers on every reserve in British Columbia but we do earnestly encourage the selection and training of qualified young native Indians by the Regina RCMP Training Division so they may return to and be authorized to police their respective reserves." Replies to both letters stated the matter would be considered, but reserve policing did not come to fruition for many years. Even then the training was not of the quality Frank had requested (see appendix 3).

It was not until many years later, after liquor and drugs had caused such havoc among the native people — in one or two cases it had resulted in murder — that Frank's suggestion was acted upon. Conditions had become so bad as a result of alcohol abuse that eight reserves in the province made an appeal to Attorney General Leslie Peterson for policing. In the BC legislature Peterson announced that special police constables, working with the RCMP, would be trained.

Frank spoke on the issue and said that a policing scheme already had been instituted for three villages on the Nass and had worked well. He noted that the constables there had not been given RCMP training, and that it pleased him the force would now be involved. Specifically, he requested that training for policing be extended to Bella Bella, Port Simpson, Kitimat, and Cowichan. The village councils in those places had already indicated they were ready to supply men for training. Ten years had passed without any authorized "on reserve" government policing and much uncontrolled violence had taken place that could have been prevented if policing had been provided sooner. Not unexpectedly, some reserves today have themselves passed by-laws prohibiting alcohol on their land.

Later that year, Premier Bennett called an election for September 19. The strategy of calling an election approximately every three and a half years instead of four was one he used throughout his time in office. In 1956, the province was prospering and he felt his party would win another mandate easily. He was correct and the Socreds were returned to power by a large majority of thirty-nine seats for Social Credit to fourteen for the CCF. The CCF remained the official opposition.

In the sweep for the Socreds, Frank Calder was one of the unfortunate members who lost his seat to Social Credit. This time in Atlin, Mr. Asselstine, the Socred, defeated him by a margin of ninety-four votes. Frank was out of office.

CHAPTER 5

The Legislature,
1956–1963

FRANK NO LONGER HAD a seat in the legislature but he certainly did not rest. He remained president of the Nisga'a Tribal Council and General Secretary of the Native Brotherhood of British Columbia. He won a province-wide First Nations election to the British Columbia Special Advisory Committee that had been established by the BC Indian Affairs Branch.

The month after his defeat Frank wrote to Andy Paul, president of the Native Brotherhood of British Columbia, asking that the Brotherhood petition the federal government to appoint a royal commission or joint committee to investigate the Department of Indian Affairs. Frank strongly believed the department was not fulfilling its mandate and should be providing better planning for living standards and better social and economic development for Aboriginal people. He stated in his letter to Paul, "There has been a laxity in the whole Indian administration since confederation and one good reason for it has been the lack of understanding on the part of the departmental personnel respecting Indian problems."[1] In his last year as an MLA Frank had completed a speaking tour across Canada, with stops in Edmonton, Saskatoon, Regina, Winnipeg, Toronto and Ottawa, and this tour had substantiated his opinion of the ministry. His main theme in every speech had been that Indians should be equal in every aspect and should be given a vote in federal elections.[2]

The federal government made a decision to hold a Canadian Indian Conference in Ottawa to address some outstanding problems. Frank had been chosen by the First Nations to represent British Columbia and the Yukon. In Ottawa he met with chiefs and delegates from across the country.[3] Discussions about the implementation of the Indian Act, and changes to the definition and registration of Indians were important agenda items. Indian lands, money, intoxicants, enfranchisement, education, health issues and economic development were all included. In a speech to the delegates, Frank said, "The government will come to realize that given the opportunity, the Indian can become self-determining, self-supporting and self-governing. . . . It will be after I go to the happy hunting ground but I predict that the time will come when the Indian will stand on his own two feet." The conference was covered internationally in the Canadian edition of *Time* magazine in December 1955, and his words were reported there.

Shortly after returning from Ottawa, Frank wrote the Nass River brief on the BC northern fishing industry. Fishing was a business Frank understood well. His family had always been fishers and he had gill-netted from the age of twelve. He began with his brother-in-law, Walter, and continued throughout his years of education. On Union steamship trips to school he had watched thousands of tins of salmon being loaded all up and down the coast. After leaving university he had worked full time at the fish cannery in Prince Rupert. No one knew better than he how important the industry was to the economy of the province.

The Calder brief on Nass fishing, was presented first to the Skeena management committee of the Department of Fisheries in Prince Rupert.[4] He began by praising the hard work and conservation measures the committee had implemented for the betterment of the salmon industry. "However," he continued, "closure for almost all of August is unacceptable because it will create great hardship for the Indians."[5] He protested the many regulations involved and proposed that the boundary for Skeena River fishing be pushed out further into the ocean. He wanted the federal government's approach to be one of "immediate control to guard against abuse in the mid-Pacific." He believed that Canada was spending time and money for the conservation of salmon, not for Canadians but for mid-Pacific fishers. He called for stricter international controls, fish sanctuaries and the sharing of conservation costs with Alaska. He claimed that "the answer to improved salmon conservation lies not in further restrictions to Canadian fisherman but rather to implementing an international agreement that governs the fishing areas of the mid-Pacific by extending the conservation boundary further west. A salmon sanctuary needs to be created in the mid Pacific."[6]

Boundaries were not changed but his brief did manage to get the number of fishing days for the year extended, and ultimately the department allowed four days fishing in June, thirteen days in July and six in August. The next year he argued against the Frobisher smelter being located in Prince Rupert because of potential harm to fish spawning. Throughout his career, Calder championed the preservation and improvement of fishing stocks for Canadian fishers. It was an issue to which Frank would return time and time again during his career.

———— ∞∞∞ ————

Almost exactly three years had passed since Calder had lost his seat in the legislature. When Premier Bennett called an election for September 1, 1960, Calder was the first candidate to be nominated and was the unanimous choice of the CCF caucus in the riding of Atlin. Frank campaigned hard throughout the riding, and this time won by a large margin. The final vote was 444 for Calder to 267 for Asselstine. Although the Social Credit party remained in power with thirty-two seats, the CCF increased their numbers by six to sixteen and continued as the official opposition. The Liberals and independents combined were reduced to four. Frank would not lose another election until the one in 1979 that initiated his retirement.

Now approaching his mid-forties, Calder was no longer "the baby" in the legislature. His appearance had changed as well; he was not as lean and athletic as he had been when he had first run for office. He had remained a bachelor and consequently tended to eat many meals in restaurants and often had dinner out with friends of both sexes. He was always careful of his appearance, however, and dressed well. Now, no stranger to politics in British Columbia, he spoke in the legislature with a strong but polite voice and continued to press for causes important to First Nations people and to all who lived in the northern regions. "We don't want condescension. We want equality" was his constant, campaign message.[7]

During the time Frank had served on the Indian Affairs Advisory Committee, he had several times asked the Native Brotherhood to request an investigation of the Federal Department of Indian Affairs. There had, however, been little change. Now, almost four years later, Frank vented his frustration in the legislature thus, "The department [federal Department of Indian Affairs] is nothing but a dumping ground for ex-colonels, ex-mayors and ex-RCMP officers whose hands are tied from advancing the cause of the Indians by Ottawa's pencil-pushing, paper-shuffling bureaucrats." He wanted Ottawa to transfer control of Indian Affairs to the provinces where there would be local input and better understanding of the problems. In March of 1961 he led a delegation of the Nisga'a Tribal Council to Victoria to lobby for this and other changes. He pressed BC to take full jurisdiction of the Indian portfolio so change could be made with greater ease and more sympathy. In return, he said, "The Indian must accept responsibility. The Indian must work hard to obtain equal status."[8] He believed reserves were nothing but breeding grounds for apathy, dependence and inferiority complexes, that they smacked of government paternalism, and should not be allowed to exist indefinitely. The sooner they were abolished, the better.

Shortly afterwards Calder was re-elected as president of the Nisga'a Tribal Council. Under his guidance the council fostered a second resolution asking for transfer of Indian Affairs to the provinces. This time it was sent to Federal Justice Minister, Lionel Chevrier. It was an in-depth follow-up to the earlier submission by the Brotherhood asking for the same amendment. In a letter accompanying the request Frank wrote a

The Nisga'a Tribal Council's delegation in Victoria, March 9, 1961 (James Gosnell, Hubert Doolan, Chester Moore, Frank Calder, Red Robinson, William McKay, Roy Azak).

rationale, specifically for BC, saying, "Indians of British Columbia are in a separate category [because they have not signed treaties] from other Indians in Canada. Therefore, they should be governed equally with other [provincial] citizens in matters of education and social welfare."[9] He had spoken because he felt the cause needed clarification and hopefully would enlist support from the province.

He illustrated the vast misunderstanding and paternalistic attitude shown to Aboriginals by telling the story of seven Nisga'a Indians who went to Victoria to press their land claim rights. Ned de Beck, clerk of the legislature, met them and spoke to them in Chinook, which de Beck believed would be the only way in which he could communicate with them. De Beck was not alone in his opinion. His ability to speak Chinook was the main reason the government had hired him. The Nisga'a, however, could not understand a word he said. The languages they spoke were Nisga'a and English. Frank told the story to the legislature as an example of the lack of understanding about present-day First Nations people. He considered the assumption that Aboriginals still spoke Chinook — a simplistic language of trade that had been developed out of necessity during the early years of European contact — to be completely demeaning. Even at the time Frank was born in 1915, it had almost died out. English had become the dominant language of trade.[10] All members applauded his speech. But it was pointed out that the transferring of Indian Affairs to British Columbia would require a change in the BNA Act, which made the change difficult.

The next year, new fishing regulations were again causing heated protests, and again Frank took up the cause. Fishing rights were a prime concern to those in the north because many depended on them for their living. This year the northern fishing season had been cut to a miniscule nine days in total. The Nisga'a council strongly objected to the harsh regulation. It took eighteen to twenty-six days fishing to provide enough fish to can seventy thousand cases of salmon, which was the absolute minimum to make the existing cannery at the mouth of the Nass viable.

In the house Frank protested, "Nine days is based only on an assumption and shows complete disregard for the economics of the area. Nine days will not allow either fishermen or canneries to meet their costs. Southern fishermen are permitted to fish until November 30 but areas north of Cape Caution are closed by mid-September. Conservation measures have been in place in the Skeena District for twenty years. Will the fisheries department tell us how much it has spent on conservation over that period and what has been accomplished? Surely there must be some improvement after so many years."[11]

At the same time Frank called for a scientific study of toxic wastes going into rivers that were spawning grounds for fish. He suggested that the waste from pulp mills might be affecting spawning and therefore fish stocks. It resulted in the Pollution Control Act being passed to regulate the dumping of sewage and industrial wastes including pulp mill waste into watercourses. In the end Frank managed to have the number of fishing days in the north increased but did not get the number that the south enjoyed.

The same month Frank again presented his Bill of Rights in the legislature. He wanted full citizenship and economic parity for everyone. He asserted that "the Indians can look after themselves given the chance," and he went on to point out that at the present time inequality exists in the following areas:

- Health care: "for many Indians and others in the north it is poor";
- Education: "Indian children should have the same opportunities as other Canadian children. There are few Indian children enrolled in public schools";
- Administration of Liquor laws: "the question of whether the consumption of liquor is good or bad should not enter into it; laws should be the same for every one";
- Housing: "for Indians and many in the north it is expensive and inferior."

On January 1, 1965, the federal government agreed to pay social welfare benefits to Indians equal to the provincial benefit they would receive if they met the eligibility requirement for provincial benefits. One of Frank's crusades had succeeded, but what he really wanted was for the province to pay them directly, not the federal government. He believed that equality meant exactly the same treatment in all respects.[12]

Year after year he reintroduced his Bill of Rights, and year after year the Socreds and Liberals voted it down. In this session he rose after the vote and pointed out, "When I first came to the house, everyone said nice things about having an Indian MLA. But when I introduced a bill similar to this it was refused on the grounds that Ottawa must pass such a bill first. Almost two years ago, in 1960, Mr. Diefenbaker's government passed The Bill of Rights for all Canadians so now other excuses are found."

In 1963, a federal election had been held and the Liberals under Lester Pearson replaced the Conservatives. As part of their election platform, the Liberals had promised a Federal Land Claims Commission. Accordingly, a few months later, the Nisga'a Tribal Council, under Calder's guidance as president, took their first, concrete step towards addressing the issue of Aboriginal title to land with the new Land Claims Commission. They passed a motion to form a united voice with the Native Brotherhood of British Columbia and the North American Brotherhood and make presentations to the soon-to-be-appointed Federal Land Claims Commission. A month later in Terrace, at a combined convention of Aboriginal associations of British Columbia, a resolution was passed to support such presentations by creating a paid, full-time position to advocate their cause. The concern for rights to their land had never vanished and was always uppermost in the minds of the Nisga'a and many other First Nations.

In 1963 compensation for holding public office was minimal. At that time elected members received $5,000 per year and Premier Bennett $15,000.00. The huge riding of Atlin cost Frank almost half his annual remuneration to make one circle of the entire region. Along with many others, he was feeling pinched, and he decided to speak out. That year in January, Frank stood in the legislature and asked the body to pass increased compensation for all members.

He said, "Quite a lot of members are afraid to speak out but I'm not. . . . I'm broke and the situation has become embarrassing. . . . In fact, I'd still be paddling my way here if it wasn't for my sympathetic banker.[13] In return, he received a riot of laughter from the house followed by a roar of applause, and even the cabinet ministers thumped their desks. Premier Bennett rose and replied that he would take the matter under consideration with the minister of finance. WAC Bennett held the offices of both premier and minister of finance. Again there was much laughter, but salaries were soon increased.

This session of the legislature was drawing to a close but Frank had one last request for his riding. In February he had asked that the road to Telegraph Creek be kept open all winter. The people, he said, "work at Cassiar in mines and on construction. The children go to school in Whitehorse, Fort St. John and Dawson Creek. In summer, they return home for weekends and doctors' visits and groceries are brought in but in winter they are isolated." He called for a highway camp to be constructed on the road to keep it clear all year. At the same time he repeated his request for air ambulance service for the north.[14]

At this point before a response to Calder's complaint was made, Premier Bennett called an election, following his pattern of holding one every three years instead of waiting until four or five had passed. Frank agreed with his party that this was a wasteful practice and an abuse of public funds. Fixed election dates would be a better way. However, the Socreds held power. The election was set and would take place on September 30, 1963. There would be one change on the ballot. In October of 1961 the CCF convention had voted to change the name of their party to the New Democratic Party (NDP).[15] Frank had attended and supported the change, and for the first time would campaign under the new banner.

He won an easy victory in Atlin, with 549 votes to Asselstine's 308 for Social Credit. The totals in the house at the final count changed very little and stood at Social Credit thirty-three, NDP fourteen, and Liberals five.

CHAPTER 6

The Legislature, 1963–1966

THE TWENTY-SEVENTH SESSION of the legislature opened on September 30, 1963. It would prove to be a session concerned with tragic occurrences requiring strong parliamentary action. Calder was closely involved and as always spoke for his northern constituents. Roads, electricity rates and, above all, safety to avoid future loss of life would be his main topics of concern in the house.

As the session opened, Calder again brought to the fore the extremely high cost of electricity in the north when compared to rates charged in the south of the province. Frank believed the injustice was affecting economic development in his riding. In each of the last two sessions, he had hoped to right this imbalance by calling for BC Hydro to take over Northern British Columbia Power. He repeated his request in this session and finally negotiations were undertaken. In a surprisingly short time they proved to be successful.

In February, the minister of mines, Mr. Donald Brothers, announced that the matter had been settled satisfactorily. It was solved by BC Hydro buying excess power from Alcan's huge aluminum project at Kitimat to meet the area's increased need, as well as by Hydro purchasing the Northern British Columbia Power Company for four million dollars. Rates became more equitable throughout the province.[1] Late the next fall a luncheon and ceremony was held to celebrate the acquisition, and Frank was one of the notables invited.

Another long-fought battle for Calder had been the construction of a highway connection between Stewart and Cassiar. He was pleased with the report in this session saying that work had been progressing well on the highway, and that in two years, in 1965, the road would be opened to a limited amount of traffic. Three years later, in 1968, it would become accessible to all-weather traffic. The cost would exceed two million dollars but Frank considered it a good expenditure.

Now that the Stewart-Cassiar Highway was becoming a reality, Frank revived another long wished for dream — a highway to the coast. He stood in the house and urged the members to pass legislation to establish an additional link that would make a new highway accessible to the Pacific by building a connection to the Stewart-Cassiar. He was gratified when the legislature agreed and announced plans to complete the coastal thoroughfare. The new route would connect Highway 1, the Alaska Highway to Watson Lake, with Highway 37, the Stewart-Cassiar to Kitwanga, where it would meet Highway 16, which takes traffic either to Prince Rupert or Prince George. Colloquially, it was referred to as the coast highway even though the deep inlets and rough terrain prevented it from following a route close to the ocean.

When all the connections were finished it would mean that travellers from the north would be able to drive from the Alaska Highway to Stewart, then to Terrace and Prince George where they could take Highway #97 to Ashcroft, where it meets the Trans-Canada Highway to Vancouver. Frank stated that as a result of the Stewart-Cassiar completion some forty mining companies had started development. It gave Frank great satisfaction, not only because at last his long years of advocacy had come to fruition, but because of the economic benefits he was certain it would bring to the north. The link to the Alaska Highway would benefit not only Canada but also the United States by enabling truck and car

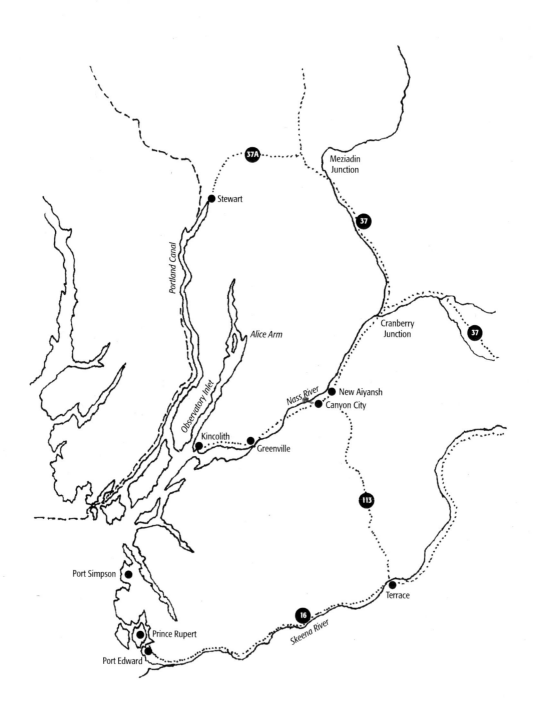

Map of the Nass and Skeena River Basins with the highways
connecting the various centres.

traffic to travel all the way from the British Columbia-Washington border to Alaska. Access would encourage many new enterprises to open.[2]

Road construction everywhere in BC was costly and difficult because of mountainous terrain and extreme weather conditions. Calamities such as landslides, avalanches and floods are common throughout the province, but seldom do they occur with the frequency or intensity of early 1965. BC's mountainous terrain hosts steep slopes in which treacherous faults are sometimes hidden. Heavy precipitation in the form of rain on the coast causes mud slides, while heavy snowfalls in the interior trigger avalanches. Strong Pacific storms and seismic activity are common in the region and often serve as catalysts.

On January 9 of that year, in the valley a few kilometres east of Hope, one of the province's most dramatic tragedies occurred. About seven o'clock in the morning, a minor earthquake caused the entire top of a mountain to break away, and with a roar equal to the combined din of hundreds of thunderstorms, surge downward. A mixture of boulders, earth, snow, trees and rubble poured onto the floor of the valley burying it to a depth of seventy metres. In the process it covered several kilometres of the Hope-Princeton highway. Three vehicles were buried and four people killed. Two were never recovered.

Interesting vignettes are still told about this tragedy. A librarian in Victoria, who lived in the area at the time, says the slide happened in two parts. A truck driver saw a first small slide, stopped in time and waited. He flagged down other cars and told them he believed it was dangerous to proceed but some did not believe him and drove headlong into disaster. He stopped others and saved them, and as such is an unsung hero. A second story is that, after two people were so deeply buried they could not be recovered from their cars, a psychic came forward and offered to show authorities where to excavate to find them. Mr. Gaglardi, minister of highways, refused, saying that the slide would stand as an honorable gravesite for them. A few months later a new highway route around the slide was constructed. Today, greatly improved, it is still in use and stands fifty-five metres above the former ground level.[3]

In the legislature members had sat hushed. Their disbelief and dismay increased as news item after news item circulated through the house.

Many rose to offer condolences and sympathy for all who had been affected by the catastrophe. Frank was one who took a more practical approach, and his words proved to be prophetic. He stood in the house and said, "Slides are a recurring disaster in my area and heavy snowfalls this winter point to an increase in avalanches and floods this spring so an emergency system should be organized on a permanent basis."[4]

Ironically, it was only three weeks after Frank's speech on emergency safety measures that a second disaster occurred. It resulted in even greater loss of life, and this time it happened in Calder's riding. When Frank had spoken in the legislature and said, 'This year's snow pack is far above normal," he could not have foreseen what was yet to come. In a single week in February a full sixteen feet of snow fell on the area north of Prince Rupert. Usually, snowfall in the area was heavy but averaged less than ten feet in total. Sixteen feet in a week was absolutely unheard of.

The Granduc copper mine, some 160 kilometres north of Prince Rupert, had a glacier situated above it. Snow massed on the ice until the weight of the enormous accumulation could bear no more. It fractured, split and crashed onto the mine below. Out of the workforce of 140 men, forty were buried. A "mayday" was immediately radioed but no help could be rendered. The weather was bitterly cold and winds blowing at over one hundred kilometres an hour made seas so heavy that they prevented the RCMP stationed in Alice Arm from going to their aid. The same weather system prevented air rescue from Vancouver or Victoria from sending assistance. Eighteen of the forty who were buried died, and the remaining twenty-two were injured. Fortunately, at the time Dr. Veasny along with a first-aid attendant was at the mine on a routine visit. Otherwise the number of lost lives may have been much greater. Even so, the loss of life was one of British Columbia's greatest catastrophes.[5]

On the floor of the legislature, Mr. Gaglardi announced that as soon as planes were able to leave, space would be reserved for Donald Brothers, minister of mines, and Frank Calder, the member for the riding. A few days later both flew to the horrific scene. Afterwards, when they spoke of the damage, they said they found it far worse than anything they could have imagined. Brothers was quoted in the *Vancouver Sun* newspaper as saying, "It is a scene of tremendous destruction and desolation. It is unbelievable." The mine was never reopened because the landscape was considered so treacherous that safety for miners could never be assured.

While it was a bad year for British Columbia with this great loss of life, there was a silver lining because Frank's request for a permanent emergency service was implemented. In addition to rescue operations, it included a surgery division at the Stewart hospital, a service that had long been needed.

In spite of the shock and disbelief that followed the two unprecedented tragedies in the province there were more mundane yet important issues on the horizon. One particular enterprise Frank supported was an Aboriginal logging endeavour. A year earlier in April of 1964, the Nisga'a villages along the Nass, with Calder's support, had formed the Pacific Logging Company and had begun to log timber from their reserve. The purpose of forming the company was to provide jobs for the Nisga'a people to augment their incomes from the declining fishing industry. However, the timber to which they had access on their reserve was dwindling fast. To make their business viable they needed access to a larger tract. Accordingly, at a timber rights hearing in Prince Rupert, the Nisga'a presented a brief asking for the right to compete with other logging companies for tree farm licenses to log crown lands. Frank was present and argued on their behalf: "If they can prove themselves in this endeavor other bands may follow. . . . The Indians must assume responsibility for self support, self-determination, independence and self-government."[6] Frank had persuaded the Nisga'a Pacific Logging company to put these ideals into practice but to do so they had to be allowed to compete for timber rights on an equal basis with other logging companies. In spite of their plea, however, and even with the support of their MLA, the right to bid on timber was denied.[7] Frank was disappointed with the outcome and considered it unfair but there was nothing further he could do at the time.

When autumn arrived, Frank made his usual complete tour of his riding during which he presided at the Nisga'a Tribal Council. Land claim presentations had become the major topic of discussion. The Nisga'a had acted on their commitment to present land submissions to the newly formed Land Claims Commission in Ottawa, but little action had resulted. However, a court case the previous spring had been closely followed by Frank, and the decision had given Aboriginals new hope. It seemed possible the outcome might have a direct bearing on the historic land rights of native people who had lived under British jurisdiction.

The case had been presided over by Judge Swencisky in Nanaimo on Vancouver Island, and involved two First Nations men, Clifford White and Johnny Bob, who had been convicted for shooting game on crown land out of season. Thomas Berger, a bright young lawyer who was already making a name for himself, defended the men. After reviewing all the facts and hearing the defence, Swencisky ruled that a three-hundred-year-old Proclamation that Berger had found — stating that Indians could hunt and fish over unoccupied land — was still valid in law. He quashed the previous conviction of the two men. Swencisky's judgment included the following crucial sentences: "The BC Game Act [that prohibited hunting out of season] is fully constitutional but the proclamation made by King George III in 1763 gave Indians the right to hunt for food and is still in effect. I hold that the agreement between the Vancouver Island Indians and the crown was a solemn document with all the status of a settlement contract."[8]

The decision elated Frank. He had spent many hours researching land title information in the archives and in the BC legislative library. From what he had seen, he was persuaded that the Swencisky decision was a significant victory. Frank had learned that the British system recognized Aboriginal land rights over unoccupied land, and the decision in this case upheld his belief. He believed it should have a favourable bearing on the Indian land claims case the Nisga'a were planning to present before the newly formed federal Indian Land Claims Commission. Another effect of the case was that the Nisga'a decided to retain Berger as their legal advisor to fight for their land claims issues.

Although land claims were the uppermost concern of the Nisga'a, they also had many unmet needs on a daily basis. Their economic situation was pitiful, and Frank considered it dire. In March of 1965 he proposed an Indian Economic Development Board for British Columbia, consisting of a social scientist, an economist, a town planner, an engineer and some Indian leaders. He said the board should have four major aims:

– Develop the resources of the reserves;
– Promote business enterprises on reserves;
– Promote employment for Indians;
– Provide research facilities.[9]

Declining fish stocks were another problem that had a damaging effect on everyone in the riding of Atlin. In February 1966, Frank spoke in the house, saying, "British Columbia has an outstanding reputation all over the world for salmon, halibut and other deep water fish. It's high time we did something about this. . . . Canada has become weak in the protection of its fisheries. Even though Canada has one of the best conservation systems in the world, the federal government has been very weak at international conferences. The U.S. has practically depleted its own fish except from the high seas. There are Japanese and Russian boats right on our own doorstep. It's time Canada spoke up and fought for fishing rights in the same way it is fighting for jurisdiction of offshore mineral rights."[10] This was a point Frank had made several times. It was becoming ever clearer to him that foreign fishers were encroaching on fish that Canadian taxes were paying to conserve.

An election was looming and for many months there had been dissension in the legislature over redistribution of seats. The ridings in the north were geographically huge but the number of voters few. Southerners felt their votes counted for less than northerners' votes. People in the north countered that if their vast areas did not receive representation they would be dominated by the south and lose a local voice to protect their people and resources. In total, there were fifty-two seats in the house and only seventeen of them were allotted to the lower mainland where fifty percent of the population resided.

A Royal Commission that became known as the Angus Commission was appointed to study the situation and recommend a more equitable distribution. After some months the commission made its report and produced a plan to increase the total number of seats from fifty-two to fifty-five. As well, it reduced the number of seats in the north-central area by three and distributed six extra seats to the large population centres in the south. When the Socred cabinet received the report, it was not entirely pleased with its contents. Members whose ridings would disappear were angry.[11] Premier Bennett sided with them and agreed to protect the northern seats. He then presented his own redistribution of seats to the legislature.

Immediately, the NDP and Liberal opposition members charged him with "gerrymandering," saying the government was only protecting the north because it would lose seats if those ridings were reduced. A firestorm erupted in the house. On the first of March 1966, a battle raged that lasted throughout the day and into the night. Finally, late in the evening Premier Bennett had had enough. He left the house and sent a message to Phil Gaglardi to adjourn the debate. A vote in the legislature was taken a few days later and the amended bill passed by twenty-nine votes to nineteen. Four Social Credit members, whose ridings would be affected, voted against it along with the entire opposition except for one, Frank Calder. He stood against his party — as he had in the past over the appointment of a senator — and he voted with the government. He believed the north had unique problems and deserved representation. Others, even some in his own party, charged it was because, if the Angus Commission's Report had been implemented in its original form, the boundaries of his riding would have changed substantially.[12]

Following his usual pattern of holding an election every three years, Premier Bennett called one for September 12, 1966. The Social Credit party was returned to power with thirty-three seats, the NDP sixteen and the Liberals five. Frank won his biggest victory ever receiving 60 percent of the vote in Atlin.

CHAPTER 7

Housing and the Legislature, 1966–1967

WHEN THE TWENTY-EIGHTH session of the legislature opened in 1966 there was little change in the distribution of seats in the house. But Social Credit had suffered one significant loss: Robert Bonner had been defeated in the riding of Point Grey. He had been the party's attorney general since the Socreds had first been elected in 1952. Premier Bennett very much wanted him to continue in the position. To this end, William Speare, who had won the riding of Cariboo Central for the Socreds, was persuaded to resign, and this allowed Bennett to call a by-election in which Robert Bonner would be a candidate. A hotly contested campaign followed in which Frank Calder played an important role.

The Nazko First Nation reserve was part of Cariboo Central but few if any of the Nazko voted. The NDP seriously wanted to win the by-election, and Frank believed that if the Nazko people could be persuaded to vote they might swing the election in the NDP's favour. The party agreed. Another factor the NDP considered favourable was the widespread disillusionment with Bonner. To many he appeared overbearing.

He brooked little if any opposition, which had led not only to his defeat in Point Grey but to general unpopularity throughout the province. A third factor the party was depending on was that Social Credit had failed to follow through on a promise to build a bridge across the Fraser River at Quesnel, the city at the centre of the riding. As a result the NDP held high hopes of winning an upset.

Hartley Dent, a man sympathetic to Aboriginal causes, was selected by the NDP as their candidate to oppose Bonner. Frank Calder and Tom Berger were designated to get out the First Nation vote. The party threw strong support behind the team, and even the National Party leader, Tommy Douglas, came to the riding to speak.

The remote Nazko Reserve, situated seventy miles west of Quesnel, could be reached only by a dirt road. Nevertheless, it represented some eleven hundred votes. Travelling there with Hartley Dent, Frank tried to prepare the candidate for the poverty he would encounter. Frank had visited many reserves in British Columbia, but from what he had been told, he was convinced that the Nazko reserve would be worse than most others he had seen. Their trip ended in a ramshackle village that consisted of a small general store and café, a little church and a one-room school. Most of the houses in the village were situated at some distance from the church and school; they were a motley collection of poorly maintained log cabins. The only building that was bright and modern was the teacher's house.

Calder and Dent needed information about the village in order to decide how best to approach the Nazko people. They asked the school-teacher about conditions on the reserve. She told them, "My house has the only hot and cold running water and the only septic tank. It has the only bathtub. The natives are filthy and it's no wonder because they make do with one well and a pump. The floors of their houses have as much mud on them as the ground outside. No one knows where the chief is. He went to Quesnel months ago and has not returned. They think he may have drowned."[1] She told them there was only one band member who could speak English and read and write well. This was Philip Patrick. Calder found him, and Philip agreed to act as interpreter. A meeting was called for the entire village. Dent spoke first and everyone listened attentively.

When Frank was introduced wearing a blue blazer, grey pleated trousers and a clean shirt with a striped tie, the Nazko found it hard to believe he was a Nisga'a who had lived on a First Nations reserve. Having never met an Aboriginal that dressed well, they were slow to accept him. With Philip interpreting, Frank spoke to them for an hour, emphasizing how important it was to vote and explaining how having Dent, who was sympathetic to their causes, in the provincial legislature, would help them. Slowly they began to nod and heed his words. "Dent" was the word Frank reiterated over and over again as the one to make an X beside. Going to a voting station and putting an X beside the name they wanted to represent them was a novel experience for most Nazko.

The by-election, though hard fought, ended with Bonner retaining the seat for the Socreds. He received 47 percent of the vote to Dent's 40 percent. The remainder was split between the Liberals and independent candidates. Cariboo Central had been considered a safe seat for the Social Credit, and even though the NDP had not won, they had come much closer than anyone expected. Much of the credit was due to the Aboriginal vote. It was a moral victory for the NDP party and even more so for the Nazko Nation. Even though their man had not won, they had taken a giant step forward in political awareness.

The next month in October 1966, the Nisga'a Annual Tribal Council meeting was held in Port Edward. It would prove to be a long provocative session with the discussion of many problems. Calder, as president, presided. Arthur Laing, federal Minister of Indian Affairs, W.R. Hourston, federal Director of Fisheries for the Pacific Area, and Thomas Berger, now a newly elected NDP MLA for Vancouver Burrard, attended. It was an impressive assembly and one that Frank hoped could be convinced to support increased Aboriginal fishing rights and land claims. He was beginning to recognize a growing relationship between the two issues.

In spite of his new position as MLA, Thomas Berger had continued as counsel for the Nisga'a, and his legal progress report was eagerly awaited. Berger spoke to the assembly, and after outlining the legalities of the case, ended on a high note by saying, "Enough progress has been made that next year in 1967 we will file a land claim on behalf of the Nisga'a in the Supreme Court of British Columbia." Along with all the Nisga'a, Frank was gratified by Berger's progress. Frank believed that if a fair land claim settlement could be attained, then equality in all areas would slowly follow.

Berger's promise that he would be able to take the Nisga'a land claim to the BC Supreme Court also made Calder realize that they would have to begin seriously raising money to pay for the expensive court action. But all this came just at the time when declining fish stocks were reducing the Nisga'a fishing catch and as a result lowering their incomes. Since donations were necessary from all Nisga'a to support the expensive legal action, it made fishing rights a thornier point of discussion than usual at the council meeting. There was heated debate but there appeared to be no short-term solutions to the problem. With some resignation, Frank agreed to put forward a motion to stop mid-Pacific fishing altogether. It called for the federal government to have signing nations of the North Pacific Fisheries Treaty agree to no salmon fishing at all in the mid-Pacific. He also called for a scientific study of toxic wastes seeping into spawning rivers. Essentially, it was the same proposal, although more elaborate, that he had put forward in his "Nass River Brief" of 1957. Director Hourston, on his return to Ottawa, once again took the issue to the federal government but as in the past no concrete change resulted.

The situation remained unresolved, and four years later resulted in an outright conflict erupting between fishing boats off the Northwest Coast. Numerous clashes between Russians and Canadians were reported. The situation grew dangerous enough that Ottawa formed a committee to negotiate a pact to settle the matter. Frank was appointed to the committee and, after a number of bargaining sessions, an agreement was reached. Canada agreed to stay off an area of the high seas about four hundred and eighty kilometres north of the Queen Charlotte Islands (now Haida Gwaii); in return the Russians contracted to stay off the "big bank" area of Vancouver Island. It was acceptable to both sides, and the United Fishermen and Allied Workers Union voted in favour of it. Frank, as well as being a good speaker, got along well with people and it helped make him a successful negotiator.

Even though he had helped to set the terms of the agreement, Frank did not believe it was inclusive enough. Back in the house he asked, "What about other nations? What do we do when the South Koreans move in where the Russians have moved out? . . . The only real solution would be to bring all Pacific-rim countries into an agreement."[2] In short, Frank believed that the agreement would solve short-term problems but long-term problems would remain. Moreover, the Alaskan fishing boats continued to fish very close to the border of the panhandle.

A second thorny issue had arisen at the 1966 Nisga'a Tribal Council meeting, this time regarding Aboriginal housing. It began with James Gosnell who, in the future, would succeed Frank as president of the Nisga'a Tribal Council. He rose and spoke about the present-day poor housing for Aboriginals. What the native people needed was better housing, he said. He also pointed out that one of the problems standing in the way of native peoples being able to apply for such housing was the fact that "circulars to Indians are written in professional language and are not understood by unprofessional people." The people simply could not decipher the bureaucratic forms they were being asked to fill out.

Throughout Canada, native housing was becoming an increasingly contentious issue. Many families had only dilapidated log cabins or shacks made of cheap wood covered with tarpaper. At times they consisted of only one room with a wood stove for cooking and heating. It was worse in some places than others depending on the means of income available to different Aboriginal groups — as Frank had seen with particular clarity at the Nazko reserve. Many Nisga'a and other Northwest Coastal First Nations people worked in the fishing or mining industries and received respectable, if seasonal, wages. However, even though their housing was much better than some, a substantial home remained beyond their means. The nature of the reserve system made good housing difficult for all Aboriginals, even if a high wage was earned. By law, all property on reserves was held in common by the nation. It could be sold only to the Crown. When an Aboriginal family needed a house, they could not go to a bank and apply for a mortgage. Without transferable land ownership there was no collateral to support mortgages for First Nation people.

To overcome the housing difficulty, at least in part, the federal government had been giving housing grants to Aboriginals. But these grants had seldom covered even bare essentials. In the mid-1960s the grant was

$4,000. At that time a very cheap house in Canada might be priced under $12,000 but most were closer to $20,000. Moreover, reserves were usually remote and had few services, which made construction costs on them expensive. Gosnell, supported by the council, decried the situation and after the meeting, not only was the grant for housing increased, it prompted Larry Hunter and W.R. Robinson of the Indian Affairs Department to make a clearly written statement when they announced the new housing allowance. The wording plainly said, "Indians will now be subsidized up to $7,000 for housing on reserves and $10,000 off reserves."[3]

For the few Aboriginals who earned reasonably good incomes the measure was a benefit, but for most it was still inadequate. Among those who benefited were the Calder and Clark families. In 1953, Aboriginals had been given the right to purchase land off reserves. A few years later, Phillip Calder had purchased a house in Prince Rupert. Frank had bought a little house on the Gorge Waterway in Victoria, and after his marriage it was to this home that he brought his bride. It had only a living/dining area, a kitchen, a bathroom and two small bedrooms. One bedroom he used as an office where on one wall he hung all the certificates and awards with which he had been presented over the years. It was an impressive collection.

The federal government became frustrated by ongoing criticism of Aboriginal housing, and started a building program for First Nations people in the late 1960s. Hundreds of houses were constructed that were identical small boxes, but they were built to the national building code and were far better than shacks and cabins. Unfortunately, because these houses contributed little to the personal wealth of the people to whom they were given, they were not inclined to spend effort or money to maintain the houses. Soon the houses fell into disrepair. It was not unlike what happened in large, high-rise, slum replacement projects in cities such as Chicago or Glasgow. There is little pride of ownership without title to the property on which one's home stands.

Housing was one of the reasons the Nisga'a Tribal Council continued, year after year, to ask for a change in the Veterans' Act. It was one of the most obvious factors in the unfair treatment of Aboriginal veterans after the two world wars. Frank had volunteered to serve in the Second World War but was rejected because of an old shoulder injury. However, his youngest brother Milton had fought throughout the war years. Following his brother's difficulties in becoming established on his return, Frank had seen first-hand the unfair distribution of government benefits returning veterans received.

During the two world wars over seven thousand First Nations men had served. Over five hundred of them were killed in action and eighteen were decorated for bravery. When peace was declared, Canada passed the Soldier Settlement Act after World War I and the Veterans' Land Act after World War II. The acts enabled returning veterans to purchase land with the assistance of low-cost government mortgages. In addition they gave veterans free postsecondary education. The benefits were of little use to Aboriginals because residential schools went only as far as grade ten, and reserves did not provide individual land ownership to support the mortgages offered. When in 1953 they were allowed to own land off reserves, no provision was made for the years of appreciation in housing value during the years since 1946. On their return to Canada, Aboriginals could not vote, could not own land and, if caught with alcohol, paid a fine.[4]

Frank had been instrumental in bringing this inequality to the agenda of Nisga'a Tribal Council meetings. At most meetings a resolution for equitable treatment for Aboriginal veterans was passed and submitted to federal and provincial governments, but once again a glaring injustice to Canada's Aboriginal population went largely unnoticed by the politicians and the general public.

Despite the many difficulties in implementing their policies, Calder felt the 1966 Nisga'a Council meeting that he had presided over had been especially successful. Many resolutions were put forward in addition to land claims, fishing and housing that had been long-standing issues for Frank. They included policing for the Nass, a change in the Veterans'

Act, ending log drives on spawning rivers and instituting work to replace welfare for employable young Aboriginals.[5]

The council meeting ended with a traditional native smorgasbord banquet and dance held at the civic centre. Tom Berger and the other delegates were delighted by over one hundred different dishes that had been prepared by a group of hard working Nisga'a women. Western and oriental delicacies were featured along with smoked seal, salmon, halibut and abalone.

CHAPTER 8

Canada's Centennial Year and the Legislature, 1967–1969

FRANK CALDER ROSE from his seat in the legislature early in the new year of 1967 to declare, "The existence of Indian reserves and the poverty on them is a black eye in the Canadian Centennial year. The atmosphere on reserves is sick; brought about by a paternalistic attitude towards Indians." He continued with an appeal to help First Nations by abolishing reserves and turning them into municipalities. Dr. Pat McGeer, Liberal MLA for Point Grey, praised his speech as "one of the finest speeches ever made in this house and certainly the most significant words brought here on the subject of Indian Affairs."[1] In spite of the brave words, little would change until after the land claims issue had been settled.

In anticipation of Canada's centennial, many projects to mark the event had been undertaken throughout the country. Northern communities were no exception, and Frank supported their efforts. A First Nations centennial project of a longhouse had been decided upon several years earlier in 1964. Their plan was to build a large, authentic structure in Prince Rupert that would serve as both a museum and an outlet for

First Nations arts and crafts. It was receiving support from the Columbia Cellulose Company through donations of logs and beams. But Calder also wanted the First Nations themselves to play a part in the building of the museum so that they could take pride in their accomplishment. To this end, he arranged with the Fisheries Association of British Columbia and the Columbia Cellulose Company to deduct contributions from the paycheques of First Nations employees who wanted to donate. Frank stated, "The success of this centre will depend on the complete support of northern village councils and their active participation."[2]

Today, the magnificent Museum of Northern British Columbia in Prince Rupert has been designed in the shape of a longhouse, but it was not built until the late 1980s. It is filled with priceless artifacts and native art. Nearby, an older longhouse is used for First Nation dance performances. Neither appears to be the structure planned in 1964, but the present museum stands as a lasting tribute to the efforts of the Northwest First Nations vision, to have their accomplishments and culture displayed.[3]

In June, the midpoint of BC's centennial year, Calder attended the NDP's three-day provincial convention held in Burnaby, BC. There had been rumours for some time of unhappiness with the long-time leadership of Robert Strachan. During his years at the helm he had given his best but was increasingly being viewed as tired and worn. Many members, including Frank, believed the party needed new blood. At the convention, Tom Berger's name was put forward as a rival leadership candidate, but he was late in declaring his candidacy and had little time to lobby party members. Strachan defeated Berger by a vote of 278 to 177 and continued as party leader. Frank, one of Berger's strong admirers was disappointed and hoped that at a future convention Berger might prevail.

Calder, as has been seen, had long worked for, and strongly supported the transfer of Indian Affairs to provincial authority. Two months later, the municipal affairs minister, Daniel Campbell, stated in the legislature that he believed the federal government would begin transferring some responsibilities for Indian Affairs to the provinces early in the following year. It would smooth the way for provinces to pass legislation that would allow reserves in British Columbia to attain control over their own affairs and to seek municipal status if they so desired.

Frank had always been strongly in favour of reserves being governed by a municipal jurisdiction but not all First Nations people agreed with him. Some leaders considered municipal status not to be in their best interests. Chief Sparrow of the Musqueam Reserve was among those in opposition. He believed municipal services from the nearby city of Vancouver would be too expensive for his band to purchase. Others felt there were not enough qualified Aboriginals to run a municipality, and some believed that running their own affairs as a reserve would be a preferable governmental structure.

In February 1968, Arthur Laing, federal minister of Indian Affairs, announced in Ottawa that First Nations would receive the right to manage their own affairs, even to the point of becoming a municipality.[4] However, he included one additional clause: it would only become possible to obtain municipal status if the province in which a reserve was located first passed enabling legislation. Frank stood in the house and said, "With the provision of this legal avenue there is nothing to prevent the Legislature in British Columbia from proceeding. . . . The government can pass complementary legislation to amend the Municipal Act so steps can be taken by any reserve to become a municipality." The legislation was passed, but no First Nation in BC pursued municipal status at that time. Slowly, it became more acceptable and, since the turn of the century, both the Nisga'a and the Sechelt nations have developed a form of municipal government.

The following November, the Nisga'a Tribal Council convened, again with Frank as president. Many past issues that had remained unresolved were raised but the highlight of the meeting was the progress report Tom Berger presented on the land claims case. He announced to the council that he had initiated litigation on Aboriginal land title by filing the case in the Supreme Court of British Columbia.[5] It was the first case of an Aboriginal land claim to be submitted to the opinion of a court of law anywhere in the world. To the Nisga'a, who had paid for the court action from their own incomes and were hoping for a favourable outcome, it was exciting news.

When reports of the case reached cities such as Vancouver and Victoria, the merits of the case were heatedly debated. The majority opinion appeared to be that the court action had no chance of success. Many professionals and editorial columns in newspapers across the province argued that Aboriginal land title had already been extinguished in law twice: first by the colonial governments that succeeded James Douglas, and again when British Columbia joined the Confederation of Canada. Berger, however, believed that the decision made in Nanaimo by Judge Swencisky, based on the Proclamation made by King George III in 1763, was still in effect and could be applied to the land claim case. Calder agreed.

Publicity over the case aroused the interest of Canada's National Film Board. They consulted Frank and, at his suggestion, the issue of Aboriginal land title and the importance of restoring historic land rights was prominently featured on film. The National Film Board titled the motion picture, *Time Immemorial: As Long as Rivers Flow*.[6] In the film Frank gave a speech in which he focused on ancient land possession and cited the basis in law for the case that First Nations leaders were filing in court. With his usual well developed eloquence he emphasized that if the case was successful it would have dramatic consequences not only across Canada but also throughout the world. His strong belief in the cause was evident and made his speech highly convincing to many.

Before the land title case went to court, Frank wanted First Nations unity within BC. He knew that an earlier attempt to foster such an accord had failed, so he had written a new constitution for a unified Indian Land Claims Committee hoping it would provide harmony. The new constitution had the dual purpose of giving the committee the ability to settle land claims in British Columbia and of providing action for maintaining First Nations identity. It was agreed upon and signed by the following presidents: Frank Calder, Nisga'a Tribal Council, Guy Williams, the Native Brotherhood of British Columbia, Gus Gottfreidson the North American Brotherhood, Jack Peters, West Coast Allied Tribes and Russ Modeste, Vancouver Island Federation of Natives. Each represented about nineteen or twenty bands. They became known as "the big five."

There remained some dissent, however, and among those rejecting the new constitution were John George of the Burrard Reserve, William

Mussell of the Native Brotherhood of British Columbia, Jay Victor, a former chief of the Musqueam and Benjamin Paul, councillor with the Indian Affairs Department. Unity was elusive. Those opposed argued that they wanted more input and that "the big five" were dictating to the other First Nations. The unfortunate split occurred only a short time before the case was to go to trial.[7]

At about this time, another event occurred which had an influence on the land claims movement. A proposal was put forward in the legislature to build a super port at Tsawwassen, outside Vancouver. For the port to be able to function, it would need access across the Tsawwassen Indian Reserve. Frank recognized that the province needed the port to accommodate freighter traffic for bulk imports and exports, but he was also aware that the newly formed Indian Land Claims Committee had established the principle that no First Nations land could be expropriated. To prevent serious trouble and to avoid any hostilities, Calder felt a negotiated process should be established immediately.

In the house Frank spoke to the proposal for a new port and stated it was time the people of the Tsawwassen Nation were told what was going on and that a consultation process needed to be established. He mentioned that Chief Jacobs of the Tsawwassen Nation had said, "We have not received any notification from the government about the port or for access through our lands and we know only what we read in newspapers. My people have been living on this land long before the white man came and most of us are happy here. We have jobs nearby and can make a living."[8] Frank finished his speech by saying, "They do not want their way of life interrupted." Calder was listened to and in the end a lease arrangement was negotiated. A matter that could have become very volatile was settled satisfactorily to both parties, thanks to Calder's intervention.

In June that year, Frank was gratified when another Aboriginal "first" was achieved. Len Marchand, a thirty-five-year-old member of the Okanagan First Nation, was elected to the federal parliament. Frank made a point of meeting with the new member and was instrumental in having Marchand made an honorary member of the Native Brotherhood of British Columbia. As will be recalled, Frank had done the same for James Gladstone when he had been appointed the first Aboriginal senator. The Nisga'a Tribal Council called on the newly elected Liberal government to appoint Marchand minister of Indian Affairs and Northern Development. However, others with more parliamentary experience were considered more qualified.

It was disappointing to many Aboriginals that Marchand had not been made a cabinet minister but it was a minor grievance compared to many other issues at the time. A serious complaint had been made by First Nations people that they had been unfairly treated by law enforcement officers. In the spring of 1969 Calder was gratified that the issue had been brought to the fore in the BC legislature.

Tom Berger charged in the house that repeated police brutality had taken place in the treatment of the people of the Sechelt Nation. In the house he accused the RCMP of harshness in their dealings with Aboriginals. "Everyone has the right to remain silent when arrested," he said, "yet it seems the RCMP do not extend that right to Indians." He related an incident on the Sechelt reserve of a seventeen-year-old girl arrested for drunkenness being kicked repeatedly because she refused to tell where she had obtained the liquor. Another case involved an eleven-year-old boy who, when he was caught with stolen tires, was threatened with strapping if he did not say who had stolen the tires. Again, a twelve-year-old boy questioned about a break-in was hit so hard in the face that he required medical attention. The band's agent had come to Victoria and complained to officials in the attorney general's office but the abusive actions had not stopped.[9] When Berger investigated he found that there were over thirty such complaints. Attorney General Peterson replied that the province could not direct the RCMP but that his office would continue discussions with the RCMP about the matter.

Berger had raised a problem that was prevalent in many areas of the province and one that Frank was very pleased had been given recognition in the legislature. It helped Frank's credibility and made him feel less isolated when an elected member who was not Aboriginal brought First Nations issues to the fore.

At this time, discrimination was widespread against Aboriginal people and included prejudice within labour unions. As a former officer of the United Fishermen and Allied Workers Union, Frank understood how unions operated and supported their right of collective bargaining. However, he did not support discrimination in any form. In the house he alleged: "Unions discriminate against Indians trying to break out of reserve ghettos and get jobs in industry because Indians are not accepted as members. Local mines and construction projects are particularly hard places for Indians to gain employment. . . . Even in cases where a company considers them good workers Indians are not receiving jobs, and as long as they're not receiving equality I'm going to stand on my feet in this house."[10] He received thunderous applause for his speech from the Socred benches, but his criticism was an acute embarrassment to his own party, which was closely connected to the labour unions

The point Calder made was heeded. Two years later in 1971 the issue of First Nations people being barred from membership in unions and professional organizations was again brought before the house, this time by the Social Credit government. They openly supported Frank when he claimed that one of the reasons so many First Nations and Inuit were unemployed was because they were barred from membership in labour organizations. The Minister of Agriculture, Cyril Shelford, stood and issued a warning, "I hope professional groups and unions will tackle this problem and find a solution. Otherwise the government will have to step in and do it for them. . . . When major projects are approved we [the government] should step in and institute training programs so that the Indians and Inuit can participate."[11] Shelford used the recent Pacific Great Eastern Railway expansion north of Fort St. John as a positive example because many Aboriginal people had been employed on it successfully.

Because the NDP received much of their support from unions, they strongly resented one of their own members making outspoken comments against unions. Once again, as he had done over the appointment of an Aboriginal senator and over the Angus Commission's redistribution of seats, Calder had opposed his own party. As always he stood up for what he believed was morally right even when it went again his own best interests politically. Clearly, dissension between Calder and the NDP was growing.

Spring that year was a sad time for Frank. In March 1969, his birth father Job Clark, Chief Long-Arm, had died at the age of seventy-nine. He had been an excellent chief. At the time of his death he had been retired from his position at Canada Packers. Job was the last of Frank's four parents, both by birth and adoption, to pass away. Arthur, his adoptive father, had been the first in 1939 and was followed by his wife, Frank's adoptive mother, Louisa, nine years later in 1948. Then Emily, Job's wife and Frank's birth mother, died in March 1961. She was long remembered for her valuable radio work in delivering weather reports in the northwest and had been credited with managing to get timely help for the rescue of more than one craft in trouble.

By custom, after Job's death, chieftainship would pass to his eldest nephew. However, since Job did not have a nephew by birth, his son Frank, who was his nephew by adoption, became chief. As they did for every new chief, the Nisga'a built a new house on their lands for him. Although he was appreciative of the house and stayed there whenever he visited, Calder spent very little time in it. Because of his commitments in the legislature, he was required to be in Victoria for most of the year. Of course, he always travelled north for the Nisga'a Tribal Council meeting in the fall, but between visits he delegated many responsibilities.

Later that spring the NDP held their planned leadership convention, and Frank would not only attend but would strongly advocate for the man he wanted to win, Thomas Berger. In April, the NDP caucus had put forward recommended names for leadership. Robert Strachan had decided to step down. There were three candidates selected for the race: Dave Barrett, Tom Berger and Bob Williams. Frank strongly preferred Berger for the position. Towards the end, Williams bowed out. The resulting race between Berger and Barrett was close, but ultimately Berger won by a vote of 411 to Barrett's 375. Berger was unanimously endorsed by the convention. Calder was delighted the party had chosen Berger, whom he greatly admired.

An election call had been expected since the previous January, and when Premier Bennett called one for August 1969, it was not a surprise. With Berger at the helm of the NDP, there were high hopes, but again the Socreds won a resounding majority. In fact, they received their largest number of votes ever. Berger resigned after this devastating loss, which included his own seat in Burrard, Vancouver. The final number of seats in the new legislature was thirty-eight seats Social Credit, twelve NDP and five Liberal. Against the tide, Frank won a strong mandate in Atlin. Soon after Berger's resignation, Dave Barrett was chosen as the new NDP leader.

CHAPTER 9

BC Land Title Court Cases and the Legislature, 1969–1972

DURING THE TWENTY-NINTH session of the legislature, Calder continued to work hard in both his riding and on committee work in the legislature. At the same time, an issue of the utmost importance to him was taking place in the Supreme Court of British Columbia. On January 7, 1969, Thomas Berger had filed the land title case on behalf of the Aboriginal Land Claims Committee and now it had come to trial. The plaintiffs named in the case were Frank Calder, William and Henry McKay, Anthony Robinson, Hubert Doolan, James Gosnell and Nelson Azak.

The claim stated that seven thousand square miles of land in the Nass River valley belonged to the Nisga'a First Nation. In the claim Berger did not ask for compensation but only for recognition that title had once existed and had not been extinguished. Because it was the first case of Aboriginal land title to be submitted to a court of law anywhere in the world it was being followed intensely not only in Canada but internationally. If successful, it could set a precedent in other jurisdictions.

Along with reporters and interested spectators, Calder was following the proceedings carefully. The case lasted five days and then the anxiety of waiting for the decision began. After nine months, on October 21, 1969, while the new legislature was in session, Mr. Justice Gould handed down his verdict.[1] He ruled against the Nisga'a. The statement that accompanied his judgment said that Aboriginal land title had not been recognized in 1866 when the colony of Vancouver Island united with the colony of British Columbia, nor when the province joined the Dominion of Canada, thus Aboriginal land title had been extinguished. The brave attempt by the Nisga'a Nation had failed.

Although disappointed, Frank remained intractable. Within the allotted forty days during which an appeal could be launched, the Nisga'a Council with Frank Calder in the chair, held a meeting at Kincolith. Unanimously they voted to take their case to the British Columbia Court of Appeal. Accordingly, Tom Berger filed the appeal on their behalf.

The hearing was set for March 2, 1970. A panel of three judges would hear the appeal. Berger based his arguments on fourteen points of law with which he disagreed in the original ruling, but the one that counted and was his main thesis rested on the Proclamation of King George III. Berger said that Mr. Justice Gould was wrong when he claimed it was no longer in effect, and once again quoted the ruling by Judge Swencisky in the Clifford White and Johnny Bob case.

The decision of the BC Court of Appeal was handed down in far less time than with the original case. Two months later in May, the Appeal Court announced its findings. After having listened to five days of testimony, the three Appeal Court judges unanimously upheld the verdict of the lower Court. They further stated that Indian Affairs were the prerogative of the federal government, and no matter what the provincial Appeal Court decided it would have no bearing on the case.

On learning of the Appeal Court's decision, Frank did not hesitate; he announced that the next move would be to go to the Supreme Court of Canada. Not all First Nations people agreed. The case would now be heard in federal court, not provincial. Some were concerned that, because they were "wards" of the federal government, it would be unwise to criticize that authority. They asked questions, such as "What if they refuse to pay treaty money? What if they reduce the size of our reserves?" They were afraid to anger the federal authority and risk retaliation. In spite of opposition from some quarters, Frank was determined to push forward.

Meanwhile in Ottawa, Jean Chrétien, Federal Minister of Indian Affairs, had been formulating the Statement of the Government of Canada on Indian Policy, generally referred to as the White Paper on Indian Affairs. For years the Aboriginal people had condemned Canada's Department of Indian Affairs and the bureaucratic, authoritative Indian Agents who ran their reserves and controlled their lives. Frank referred to the system as "Canada's apartheid." Even though people in Canada were appalled by the way white South Africans treated coloured men and women, they refused to recognize that Canada treated Aboriginals in many of the same ways. First Nations people were restricted to their reserves, land for which the government had drawn the boundaries. True, they were technically free to travel or work anywhere they chose outside their reserve, but in reality an Aboriginal faced many difficulties. Outside the reserves, landlords, unions, professional organizations, restaurants and government officials shunned them. The city held attractions for First Nation people, but because they could seldom find jobs or accommodation, many who travelled there joined the company of skid row derelicts.

There was increasing awareness that Canada's native people faced serious problems, that federal policies up to then had not worked. The system of reserves had done nothing but foster dependence, take away initiative and drain Aboriginals of ambition. Recognizing that something must be done, the federal government began formulating a White Paper that would attempt to address the problems.

As minister in charge of Indian Affairs, Jean Chrétien prepared the document, which was believed to reflect the "Just Society" principles of Prime Minister Pierre Trudeau. Amongst other things, the White Paper proposed the following:

- Eliminate Indian Status;
- Dissolve the Department of Indian Affairs within five years;
- Abolish the Indian Act;

- Convert reserve land to private property that can be sold by the band or its members;
- Transfer responsibility for Indian Affairs from the federal government to the provinces and integrate these [provincial] services into those provided to other Canadian citizens;
- Provide funding for economic development;
- Appoint a commissioner to address outstanding land claims and gradually terminate existing treaties.[2]

Frank was strongly in favour of the contents of the White Paper. He had long advocated such measures and believed that First Nations could negotiate better with their own provincial governments than with distant Ottawa.[3] The federal government, however, had not consulted with any of the First Nations before introducing the paper, and not a single Aboriginal had had any input. Many First Nations considered the secret way the White Paper had been prepared, and the fact that they had been ignored, insulting. Even before it was tabled they were prepared to reject it.

Frank recognized that there were problems with the way Chrétien had introduced the White Paper and spoke seriously against the lack of consultation, but on the other hand he thought its contents should not be dismissed lightly. He hoped that with the transfer of responsibility for Indian Affairs to the provinces, First Nation funds would be used to introduce a municipal system of government for reserves. He recognized it would take time but he believed that, if given the chance, Aboriginals could in the end conform to the social, economic and educational standards of Canada. He believed that eventually First Nation peoples should pay the same taxes as other citizens and in return should receive the same benefits. He said, "For one hundred years we have had confinement and neglect and now there must be one hundred years of subsidized, rehabilitation programs." As always, his ultimate goal was absolute equality for everyone.

In October, Frank, as president of the Nisga'a Tribal Council, argued for acceptance of the 1969 White Paper at the twelfth annual convention in Kincolith. Even though he disapproved of the way it had been developed, he emphasized that the paper had much merit.[4] He carried the day and the council passed a resolution to accept the White Paper, but in principle only. There was one dissenting vote. To the press, Calder emphasized that the Nisga'a had not yet seen the detailed terms of the White Paper and that the vote had been only on the principles contained in the document. He also told the press that the Nisga'a would probably be the only nation to pass it.

Strong opposition existed to the proposals, and not only because of the secret way they had been developed, but because the new structure would require votes on major issues that could reduce the control of the present leaders. As time progressed, the paper became increasingly disliked and was denounced on every possible detail. The belief became prevalent among most chiefs that the document was nothing other than an attempt to assimilate Aboriginals and change their way of life. Most did not favour a change in the way they were governed and especially did not want a municipal form of government imposed that would encompass a universal voting system. They even objected to the title, "White Paper," as being condescending.[5]

In spite of its flaws Calder supported the intent of the paper's content. In doing so, he lost much of the long-time support he had always enjoyed from his fellow chiefs and faced serious resentment. Regardless of what it might cost him in future support, he always stood up for what he believed was right. This time, however, it was even more difficult since he was opposed by a majority of his own people, and not simply by the unions or his own political party. At the time he said that there was always a price to be paid for taking a principled position. But he never wavered. Soon that price would have to be paid in full.

—∞∞∞—

The opening of the twenty-ninth assembly of British Columbia in January 1971 was marred by social unrest. A demonstration sponsored by the BC Federation of Labour to protest the high level of unemployment in the province erupted into mayhem. It started outside, but from the grounds of the legislature protesters forced their way into the galleries of the house where they became loud, wild, rough and churlish.

Calder considered it utterly disrespectful of the democratic parliamentary process. Angrily, he stated in the house that the BC Federation of Labour should ask for the resignation of Ray Haynes, the secretary-treasurer, who had been instrumental in organizing the rally. He berated Haynes for not placing limits on the hoodlum behaviour of the demonstrators. He said, "No section of society should control MLAs whether it be labour or big companies. Anyone who sponsors that kind of rabble should be taught a lesson." Believing that the Federation of Labour was attempting to control his party, he continued, "I'm getting fed up with the public blaming the NDP every time there is a strike in this province. The NDP should stand independent of any section of society."[6] There was wild desk thumping from the Socred government seats just as there had been when Frank had attacked unions for denying Aboriginals jobs. Frank's own party sat silent; the labour movement supported the NDP both morally and financially.

The NDP publicly rebuked Frank for his stand. The executive passed a motion that was reported in the *Vancouver Sun*, as saying, "The party regrets the unwarranted attack [by Frank Calder] on the Federation of Labour in British Columbia and the labour movement generally; his words were inaccurate."[7] On the other hand, Ron Thody, editor of a newspaper in Terrace, praised "Fighting Frank," as he had come to be known, for taking a "responsible stand" on the issue. *The Vancouver Province* also supported Frank's position on the incident.[8]

A much happier event intervened that was of special importance to the people of British Columbia. 1971 was the provincial centennial year celebration: the one hundredth anniversary of BC's entry into the Confederation of Canada. For part of the celebrations Queen Elizabeth II toured the province for nine days from May 3 to 12. As Canada's head of state, she had visited the country more than twenty-two times since she first came to the throne, but this time it was especially for the people of British Columbia. Prince Philip and Princess Anne accompanied her. Among the places they stopped were Kelowna, Williams Lake, Tofino, Comox and of course Vancouver and Victoria.

At Government House in Victoria, the Lieutenant Governor, the Hon.

John Nicholson, held a formal reception in her honour. All members of the legislature were invited, and Frank felt privileged to receive his invitation along with the others. He remembered tales from the years before he was born when the Nisga'a were fighting for their land. The first Nisga'a land commission had been formed almost one hundred years ago and had sent petitions to officials in London and to the British monarchs. Often they did not know whether or not they had been received and, if they were answered, it was only from an insignificant underling.[9]

During his early life in the Nass, it would have been unthinkable to Frank, his family or any Nisga'a that one of them would actually be introduced to a British monarch or take their hand. Frank had met her when she was Princess Elizabeth but now she was the Queen, head of the entire British Commonwealth. At the reception she and her family were gracious, all took Frank's hand and spoke a few words that made it an extraordinarily touching experience for him.

A year later in 1972, a great honour was bestowed on Frank by the Nisga'a people for his tireless work on their behalf. Four chiefs, each heading one of the four clans, awarded Frank the title of "Chief of Chiefs," which had not been granted to any Nisga'a leader since 1911. He was presented with a talking stick with the four crests of the clans carved by Eli Gosnell. On receiving it Frank gave this reply, "I think it's quite rare. I find it a great honour. It's not what I was looking for but I accept it. Any chief that carries a stick like this has only the crest of his own clan on it but the one I carry has all four crests of the Nass River and the blanket you presented with it has all four as well." Later, thinking back on the honour, Frank said of the talking stick with the four crests, "It's so rare that if anything happens to me I think a museum will want it." Throughout his life, Frank valued this honour above all others because it was given by his own people in recognition of his efforts on their behalf.[10]

Shortly afterwards in the legislature, the attitude of equality that Frank strove for was never more clearly demonstrated than when Donald Brothers, Minister of Education, announced to the house that he would introduce a special curriculum for Aboriginal pupils in British Columbia. In a heated reply, Frank stood and clearly stated, "Don't you dare introduce a special curriculum for Indians in this province. . . . What is good for your child is good for the native. . . . Indians have shown that they can pass the public school curriculum and do not need any favours." He continued by saying that it was the correspondence courses that students in rural areas were forced to take after grade seven that caused the major problem. Students in remote areas found them difficult because they did not have the supervision provided by a classroom teacher and sometimes did not have parents educated enough to guide them.[11]

During the session Calder called for a Royal Commission to study effects of the reserve system on First Nations people. He wanted the Commission to hear the views of Alan Fry, author of *How a People Die*. Fry had been an Indian Agent on Vancouver Island and was very outspoken regarding how the system took away initiative and instilled feelings of inferiority in Aboriginals. Some First Nations people felt insulted by the book, but Frank, even though he did not agree with everything Fry wrote, agreed with his conclusion that the reserve system needed to be replaced. He had long said the same thing himself. Again he called for an end to reserves and received desk-thumping approval from the house.

Throughout his time in the legislature, Frank worked hard for the people of the north — as can be seen by the number of questions he asked. The British Columbia legislature, unlike the federal government, did not have a question period. However, members could question cabinet ministers through written submissions. Up until the middle of March for this session, the record holders were Pat McGeer of the Liberal Party and Frank Calder of the NDP. Each had submitted eleven questions. Calder's questions all related to his huge, wilderness riding of Atlin and the many problems that affected his constituents that often were not understood by city people.

In spite of the Social Credit's substantial majority, the twenty-ninth session of the British Columbia Legislature had not gone well for them. They had been in power since 1952 and were beginning to appear stale to the general public. The government had introduced practically no new policies. The Kootenay region was unhappy over the Columbia River Power project that had been started in the 1950s. Even though the dams were located in their region and had affected their recreational areas, there had been no direct benefits to the people living there. In addition, it was generally felt that the excess power the dams generated had been sold too cheaply to the United States. The British Columbia Teachers' Federation complained loudly because Premier Bennett had used their pension fund to finance the dams, and the bonds the fund received in return carried a very low rate of interest. There were signs of disillusionment throughout the province.

In spite of the negative factors, Premier Bennett followed his usual pattern of calling an election after three years had passed. This time, however, his practice did not meet with its usual success. The election, called for the end of August 1972, resulted in a solid reversal of fortunes. The final count of thirty-eight NDP, ten Social Credit, five Liberals and two Progressive Conservatives meant Premier WAC Bennett's reign was over. His comment on the loss was, "I guess I went to the well once too often." Frank's long awaited election majority for his party had finally arrived.

The new premier, Dave Barrett, was dynamic, hard working, a good orator and only forty-eight years old. After he had won, the newspapers showed pictures of him playing rugby. It was in sharp contrast to the defeated Socreds, led by the seventy-two-year-old WAC Bennett. Barrett projected a completely new image and the public was ready for a fresh start. Along with the rest of his party, Frank looked forward to a bright future.

CHAPTER 10

The Calder Case, 1971–1973

AFTER LOSING THE LAND title case in the BC Court of Appeal in May 1970, Frank was determined to take the case to the Supreme Court of Canada. Four factors made this extremely difficult. First, he was a busy, sitting member of the BC legislature and deeply involved in prickly issues such as the White Paper and fishing rights. Second, he did not have the unanimous support of the First Nations people. Third, he did not have the money required to take the case to the Supreme Court of Canada. Fourth, the Canadian prime minister at the time, Pierre Elliott Trudeau, had categorically rejected the idea that First Nations peoples had rights different from other Canadian citizens. He had been quoted as saying, "The government does not recognize Aboriginal title and, as a result, sees no need to enter into further treaty negotiations."[1] It was a negative backdrop against which to proceed to the Supreme Court of Canada, but nothing would change Frank's mind. He was determined to somehow get the case to the Supreme Court of Canada.

Calder had been brought up to believe in Nisga'a rights to the lands of the Nass Valley and had been educated to fight for them. He never forgot the time when he was only six years old and his father Chief Na-qua-oon, at a great feast held by the chiefs of the Nass River villages, had stood him on the table, and said: "This boy, this dream boy, I am going to send to a white area. He will learn the ways of the white man. . . . He will move that mountain." Over the years Frank had learned that changing the law on Aboriginal land title was indeed as difficult as moving a mountain. It had been a heavy burden to place on the shoulders of a young boy but he never forgot his father's words nor lost sight of the mission he had been given.

Throughout these years, Calder's own research in the legislative library had convinced him that there was a legal basis for land title, that the words from the folk song, "This Land Is Your Land," meant *First Nations* land. In the Legislature Frank had once stated, "Not even the ground on which the Legislative Buildings stand has been surrendered and we don't even get rent for it."[2]

Looking back over the Nisga'a history, Frank understood the feelings of injustice that the Nisga'a Nation had experienced when Commissioner O'Reilly had arrived and explained that the Queen now owned all their land. The Nisga'a had at no time ever surrendered their valley. In fact, Frank thought that the changes to the Indian Act of 1927 — which had forbidden fundraising for the purpose of pursuing Indian land title unless the government gave permission to do so — was evidence that the government had feared a native attempt to pursue their case in the courts. Once the section forbidding fundraising for land claims was omitted in 1958, Frank knew that the Nisga'a had immediately pursued legal right to their land.

Tom Berger agreed with Frank's assessment and believed there was strong substance for a case based on the British Proclamation of 1763 by King George III. As has already been stated, Berger had previously won the *White and Bob* case over hunting on Vancouver Island, based on the British Proclamation. He was very familiar with the document. In part, the document stated, "No Indian lands should be taken or in any way disposed of until they have been purchased by the Crown. . . . When British Dominions have not been ceded to or purchased by the sovereign of Great Britain they are considered as reserved for the natives."[3]

To go to the Supreme Court of Canada would be expensive but vital in Frank's opinion. Funding was his main obstacle. The two court cases that had been lost in BC had been paid for by the Nisga'a entirely from their own money. It was a serious loss. This was in spite of the fact that Thomas Berger, in Frank's words, "worked for a pittance." To take their case to the Supreme Court of Canada would require greater resources than First Nations could afford.

Their plight was brought to the attention of the Venerable Robert MacRae, an Anglican Archdeacon, who was sympathetic to the Nisga'a cause. He knew first-hand from his time ministering to the Nisga'a how important land was to them and understood their strong sense of injustice over losing control of their traditional territory. Dr. MacRae had been staff consultant to Dr. Charles Hendry of the University of Toronto who had developed in 1968 a report titled "Beyond Trap Lines."[4] The report was presented to the General Synod of the Anglican Church when it met the next year in Sudbury in 1969. It included recommendations to the church ministry regarding First Canadians, saying that not only should poverty be addressed but also economic development. A request for funding for land title claims was made to the Synod on behalf of the Nisga'a by John Hanon. It was passed, and as a result the "Primates World Relief and Development Fund" donated $10,000. It was not a huge sum but it was enough to enable the Nisga'a to take their case to the Supreme Court of Canada. The support of the Church of England proved to be the pivotal turning point for the Nisga'a lawsuit.[5]

As soon as he knew funding was available, Frank immediately informed Tom Berger that the case could go forward. In *Let Right Be Done*," Joseph Gosnell, a prominent elder and future Nisga'a chief, quotes Frank stating optimistically at the time, "The Nisga'a people are not on trial. The Indian peoples are not on trial. British justice is on trial. I believe British justice will prevail."[6] Frank also stated that if the Supreme Court of Canada failed him he would go to the International Court at The Hague and even, if necessary, to the United Nations. After the previous two losses, however, the overwhelming support he had initially received for his cause was evaporating. This time his opponent would not be the province of BC; it would be the federal government of Canada, the government that controlled Indian Affairs.

Frank needed all his inner strength once the case had been filed in the Supreme Court. There was much influential opposition to the case. Many First Nations people were afraid that if Calder lost again, the government would feel justified in reducing benefits they had already achieved. Most people, including those in Frank's own party, considered the cause futile and some considered it laughable. Had not title twice been extinguished by law? It was claimed that the First Nations people were so primitive at the time that they would not even have understood the concept of land title. It was assumed that because their boundaries had never been legally registered, their claims could not be proven.

Frank's popularity within his party and with the general public dwindled to an all time low. When he had stood in the house and spoken against unions barring Aboriginal workers from membership, and later against a demonstration by the Federation of Labour disrupting the legislature, he had embarrassed the NDP party. In addition, he had not done his own standing in the NDP any good when at the leadership convention he had strongly supported Tom Berger against Dave Barrett, who was now his boss. Currently, he was again embarrassing his party by continuing to fight an unpopular, apparently futile case.

In spite of all opposition, in November 1971, Frank succeeded in bringing the case of *Calder et al. v. Attorney-General of British Columbia* to the Supreme Court of Canada. As plaintiffs, Frank along with six Nisga'a who had supported him in the British Columbia cases and a few representatives from other First Nations travelled to Ottawa. The case before the Supreme Court was attracting wide media attention because it was paramount to the interests of all Aboriginal peoples, not only in Canada but also throughout the world. This time it would not be a lower court but the Supreme Court of Canada that ruled, and this made the decision especially important. A panel of seven judges had been selected to hear the case.

Five days had been set aside by the Supreme Court of Canada to hear the case of *Calder et al. v. Attorney-General of British Columbia*. The trial opened with Douglas McKay Brown, QC, chief attorney for the Crown, stating in his opening remarks that the controversy should never have reached this court. He claimed that the Nisga'a had only brought their case to Ottawa to exploit its nuisance value.

Berger disagreed and put forward an argument that involved events from the early days of British Columbia's history. He established that the Nisga'a had never willingly relinquished any of their land. On the contrary, they had always demonstrated a strong affinity for their territory. Even an early maritime trader, Charles Bishop, who had first contacted the Nisga'a at the mouth of the Nass River between 1793 and 1794, had realized the Nisga'a, were passionate defenders of their land and had recorded their passion.[7]

Thomas Berger based his claim on the fact that historically British Columbia had been a British possession. This point was vital to Berger's case. He related some of the pertinent history, pointing out how in the late 1770s both Spain and Britain had claimed the area. In 1789 Spain had established a fort at what is now Nootka. In the process, some British trading vessels were seized and Britain threatened war. In 1790 Spain and Britain, in a document called the Nootka Convention, agreed that Britain along with the Spanish would have access to trade on the coast. Two years later both countries sent commissioners to reach a final settlement of boundaries. Captain Vancouver acted for the British and Captain Quadra for the Spanish but only agreement in principle was reached. Later in 1795 the Spanish abandoned their fort and the British flag was raised. Nothing more was heard from the Spanish.[8] Clearly, since 1795 the coast had been a British possession.

Berger argued that because the coast of British Columbia had been a British possession, the 1763 Proclamation of King George III guaranteed Nisga'a Aboriginal rights to unoccupied land that had not been relinquished. Furthermore, he stated there had never been a treaty signed in BC with the Nisga'a and compensation had never been paid for any Nisga'a land in the province. The reserve system had been introduced without native consent and there had been no consultation with them regarding the "Terms of Union" between British Columbia and the Dominion of Canada in 1871. On this basis he argued that the situation contravened the Proclamation of King George III that Judge Swencisky had ruled was still in effect when he decided the *White and Bob* case.

Douglas Brown, for the Crown, countered that, at the time of the King George Proclamation, the King did not know the Nass Valley existed. He continued by saying it was almost thirty years later before Captain Vancouver arrived on the west coast of British Columbia. He declared the Proclamation had applied only to the First Nations that the British Empire had contacted up to the time of its declaration. Furthermore, Brown argued, even if title had existed at one time it had long been extinguished by legislation. And, Brown alleged, at the time of the European's arrival the Nisga'a had not been organized or sufficiently aware enough to sign a land treaty.

Berger refuted this argument by citing the fact that when Vancouver Island became a colony under Governor James Douglas, he had signed fourteen treaties with First Nations on Vancouver Island (the so-called Douglas treaties). At the time, these were recognized as following British principles of law, but were revoked when Vancouver Island joined the colony of BC. Obviously Douglas had achieved negotiation with the indigenous population and believed it was possible and necessary.

Frank testified at the trial and said, "Totems that exist to this day mark the Nisga'a claim. The Nisga'a had not developed writing but used other methods to mark their claim to land. Before Europeans arrived they had sophisticated legal concepts of their own."[9] From time immemorial the Nisga'a Nation owned the land in the Nass Valley from mountaintop to mountaintop. Other First Nations had always respected their right to the entire basin.

Professor of Law Wilson Duff, of the University of British Columbia, supported Calder's view. He told the court, "The laws the Nisga'a imposed upon the land and waters were different from those recognized by our system but were clearly defined and mutually respected."[10] The same arguments that had been used in the Supreme Court of British Columbia were reiterated and expanded upon. As had each of the first two cases, the proceedings lasted a full five days.

Finally, on January 31, 1973, five months after the NDP victory in BC, and more than a year after the case had first been submitted to the Supreme Court of Canada, the momentous result was announced. Six of the seven judges accepted the concept that the Nisga'a had enjoyed Aboriginal title before the Europeans arrived. They agreed that Aboriginal title was a concept recognized in British Common Law and as such had been accepted throughout the British Empire. On the first question of whether or not the Nisga'a historically had held land title the Nisga'a won. However, on the second question of whether or not such rights had been extinguished in law, three of the seven judges decided rights to title had been extinguished in law and three argued that such rights were still valid. The three that claimed validity did so because Canada had attempted to extinguish ownership without compensation. There was a split decision of three to three on the second part of the issue. The seventh judge abstained on both issues on the grounds that a fiat (permission from the government to sue) had not been obtained and believed the case should have been dismissed on that technicality. The tie meant the Nisga'a had lost.

The decision, written by Judge Emmett Hall was thorough in its coverage of the arguments and forceful in its prose. Even though it was not a victory, it became one for Aboriginal people. Berger saw that Judge Hall had recognized the crucial point that "Aboriginal title arises from Aboriginal ownership, possession and occupation of the land.[11] Prime Minister Pierre Trudeau on reading Judge Hall's decision was impressed and convinced enough by the arguments Berger had presented that he reversed his stand on Aboriginal land rights.[12] Even though Trudeau's government at that time was in a minority position, he brought the results of the Land Title Case before parliament and argued that Aboriginal title should be recognized — on the basis of the strong case Berger had presented. Both opposition parties agreed with Trudeau's viewpoint. A motion supporting Aboriginal land rights passed parliament by a large majority. Not only did the federal government recognize Aboriginal title but they agreed to enter into land claim negotiations. Calder's loss had been transformed into a great victory.

Prime Minister Trudeau contacted Frank and explained why and how his views had changed. Frank appreciated Trudeau's reasoning and felt truly vindicated. After his long years of leadership and tenacity, even when his cause looked hopeless, at last he had achieved success. This was

Senator Len Marchand, Frank Calder, Prime Minister Pierre Elliott Trudeau and Eli
Gosnell in a happy mood after the decision of the Supreme Court of Canada in 1973,
which caused Trudeau to change his mind about First Nation land rights.

a triumph for Aboriginal people throughout Canada. Ever after, the
court action of *Calder et al. v. Attorney-General of British Columbia* would
be referred to as the "Calder Case."

The decision led Canada's First Nations down the path of political
negotiation for their rights and compensation for the losses that they had
suffered at the hands of the federal and provincial governments. The
decision not only benefited Canadians but Aboriginal peoples everywhere. *Calder* has been cited in the courts of Australia, South Africa,
New Zealand and elsewhere.[13] It has become a model throughout the
world. *Calder* had indeed set a precedent. Compensation was yet to come,
but the mountain had at last been severely shaken.

CHAPTER 11

The Legislature, 1972–1973

"IT WAS THE BEST OF TIMES, it was the worst of times," so Charles Dickens opened his classic novel *A Tale of Two Cities*. No better phrase could be found to describe the years 1972 and 1973 in Frank Calder's life.

For the first time in his political career, Frank belonged to the party that would form the government. He had worked faithfully for his riding as a member of the Opposition for over twenty years but now at the end of 1972 the NDP had won not only victory but also a robust majority. It meant that policies in which Frank believed could be moved forward, The New Democrats had swept the Social Credit party out of office in almost all areas of the province, and Dave Barrett, the new premier, promised "a just and open government." It seemed like a new beginning.

As soon as the opening ceremonies were over, Barrett appointed his new cabinet, which consisted of only fourteen members. Compared to the previous government, it was three members smaller, and the average age was six years younger. Barrett retained the positions of both premier and minister of finance as had his predecessor, WAC Bennett. Alex

MacDonald, a long time member, also held a double portfolio as both attorney general and minister of commerce. Barrett appointed Eileen Dailly deputy premier, the first woman to hold such a post in Canada. Frank Calder received the post of minister without portfolio.

Frank was the first Aboriginal to hold a cabinet position in Canada, but it had not come without disappointment. He had served the NDP in the legislature since 1949, but his cabinet post did not reflect either his experience or long years of dedicated service. Many, particularly the native people in the province, were unhappy he had not received a more important ministry. Guy Williams, the Aboriginal senator from Kitimat who had been appointed after Gladstone's death, publicly claimed that Frank had not been given his due. Lou Desmarais, assistant to the Union of British Columbia Indian Chiefs, claimed Barrett had made Calder his "token Indian" by making him minister without portfolio.[1]

Before the election Dave Barrett had gone to the riding of Atlin and joined Frank in his campaign. In Stewart, they had announced a six-point program for the North. The party promised to do the following:

- Upgrade the road from Stewart to the Alaska Highway to an all-weather road;
- Upgrade medical facilities at Stewart Hospital and employ fulltime qualified staff;
- Institute free air ambulance service throughout the north;
- Provide equalization grants to students in isolated areas for post-secondary education;
- Encourage secondary industry in the north;
- Study the feasibility of extending the British Columbia Railway through Bear Pass to Stewart;
- Provide funds for a road and bridge at Kincolith.[2]

It was an ambitious program and one for which Frank had long advocated. Over many years he had fought for funding for all these improvements, and the soon-to-be premier publicly pledged his assistance, saying, "Calder is the only man who speaks for the north.[3] Frank was deeply gratified to receive his support. Even though the premier subsequently did not give him an important cabinet post, he had praised him publicly

Frank at the Coqualeetza reunion in 1972 with Mrs. Ruth Smith (left)
and Mrs. Ed Kelly (right), who organized the event.

and promised assistance for the huge riding of Atlin. Frank looked forward to many positive changes.

Shortly after the election, another event occurred that made the year a
good one for Frank. One morning Frank opened his mail and found that
former students at Coqualeetza were planning a reunion. Frank thought
it was a splendid idea and was pleased to attend. In fact, over one hundred and fifty former pupils and teachers were present. Coqualeetza had
undergone two transformations in the years since Frank and his brothers
and sisters had attended. When residential schools were first phased out,
it became a hospital, and at the time of the reunion it was the home of the
Coqualeetza Restoration Project.

Senator Guy Williams, the Hon. Frank Calder, provincial cabinet minister, and Mr. Solomon Wilson, successful businessman, were all prominent former students who were asked to say a few words at the gathering. Senator Williams obviously remembered the soccer games and had experienced mishaps on the field: "I remember Chilliwack as a small town with a very clannish soccer team. I still bear some of the scars from those matches." Frank remarked how important the school was to him: "I came here when I was nine years old and for thirteen very important years it was my home." He concluded by saying, "When I came here today I couldn't help but have many, many memories. I only regret that we didn't start to have these reunions sooner."

Mr. Wilson, who was then eighty-six years old, had arrived at the school in 1899. He recalled, "When I arrived at Coqualeetza I couldn't say anything more than 'yes' and 'no' in English, and my classmates had to translate for me. I was never very good at learning but what I learned here helped me a lot. When I worked on the fishing boats I handled thousands and thousands of dollars without any problem." The reunion was a great success and many thanks went to Mrs. Ed Kelly of Sardis and Mrs. Ruth Smith of Chase, former students, who had helped organize the event.[4]

As minister without portfolio, Frank had been given the job of preparing briefs on the condition of natives throughout the province. It was a long arduous job entailing many different aspects and much travel. Unknown to most, even though he was working as hard as any other cabinet minister he was receiving only $21,000 per year compared to all other cabinet ministers' salaries of $24,000. James Chabot, the Social Credit member from Columbia River, spoke in the house saying, "I wonder why government has made Calder only minister without portfolio when he has been charged with such an important task. He should be paid the same as other ministers if several serious studies of Indians in the province are to be undertaken. Why not make him, Minister of Indian Affairs?"[5]

Frank rose and replied, "Over my dead body. A provincial Department of Indian Affairs would only create more bureaucracy. This is one member who will absolutely refuse to establish another Indian Affairs Department in this country." He said that his assignment was to ensure all public services were extended to First Nations people. He agreed, however, that it was a big job. He also agreed that he should be paid the same salary as other cabinet ministers.[6] Subsequently his salary was raised accordingly, and one wonders if his originally receiving less than the other ministers resulted from some traces of remaining racism.

Frank was now more equitably compensated for his work, but he was beginning to feel storm clouds gathering around him. Today the Calder Case stands out as an iconic moment in Canadian politics, but at that time, in the early '70s, the results of the case were not popular with either the general public or his party. The fact that the federal government had agreed to negotiate with First Nations people posed grave difficulties for the newly elected BC government. The results of land resolution would affect British Columbia to a far greater extent than any other province because it had not signed treaties with its Aboriginal population, as had other provinces. If land ownership was to be negotiated, many wondered where it would start and where it would stop. Would the entire province be subject to claims? It was the first time the NDP party had been in power; they did not relish tackling in their first term what many people saw as an unpopular cause. They took the stand that was accepted by the opposition parties that all land that was privately or publicly owned was not open to negotiation. Frank did not object, but he wanted negotiations opened.

In June of 1973 the federal minister of Indian Affairs, Jean Chrétien, spoke in the House of Commons on the BC provincial government's failure to move forward on negotiating First Nations land claims. He followed up by sending a letter to Alex MacDonald, the province's attorney general, requesting that the province honour such claims. Chrétien stated, "Land that is rightfully theirs according to the Supreme Court should be returned."

Alex MacDonald replied, saying, "The federal government seems to have a problem it is trying to cast to us. Indians and the lands reserved for Indians are clearly a federal responsibility."[7] Ottawa responded that the province controlled all the land within its own boundaries and that this fact necessitated that British Columbia be at the negotiating table.[8]

The provincial government ignored Chrétien. Every member of the

NDP party recognized that this difficult problem, now squarely on their shoulders, would not exist if it had not been for Calder's tenacity in taking the land title case to the Supreme Court of Canada. This was exactly the reason the party had resisted Frank's efforts before the case was filed. The political difficulties were so ominous that it was not until 1992 when another NDP government led by Premier Mike Harcourt took office that any provincial government began seriously to negotiate.

Frank, of course, agreed with the federal government's position, and he began to lobby for his cause, spending more and more time in the Canadian capital. This was in spite of the fact that he knew this would be unpopular at home. He once led a First Nations delegation to Ottawa, and even managed a meeting with Prime Minister Trudeau, a feat not often accomplished. After that, Chrétien wrote to the BC government several times but never received a reply. Frank's position was difficult. His own people, from whom he had raised a great deal of money, wanted compensation. But an unfavourable attitude towards recompense existed in his party and, indeed, throughout most of the province.

Calder was a hard worker in the legislature but he had a private life too. He especially enjoyed dining out and frequented many of Victoria's restaurants. As a bachelor he found it pleasurable and convenient. He had a wide range of convivial acquaintances who often joined him. He found dinner and good conversation a pleasant, relaxing way to spend an evening.

On April 27, 1973, after having dinner with a woman friend from Calgary, the woman's car was noticed by the police because it was parked partially blocking an intersection. She and Frank were pulled over onto Menzies Street. The police thought that probably Frank had been driving, and he could not produce a driver's license. Frank did not have and never did have a driver's license, and he had never owned a car. He usually took taxis. Perhaps, because of the way he'd grown up, driving did not come as naturally to him as it does to most people.

During questioning, Frank became agitated and increasingly angry.

Frank Calder, circa 1973.

As a result, the car was searched and a capped bottle, partially full of alcohol, was found. The law stated it was illegal to transport alcohol unless it was sealed and had never been opened. Frank angrily shouted that it was "a set up" and the police took him down to the station. He spent the remaining hours of the night in a cell for being intoxicated, but no charges were ever laid. Later his friend from Calgary confessed that she had been driving and paid a substantial fine.

At the time, the event received barely a mention in the press. It was considered fairly insignificant and did not warrant much interest. Publicly, it was not discussed by any member of the legislature. Over two months later on July 4, Premier Barrett phoned Calder, who was in Atlin on the annual tour of his riding, and asked him about a drinking episode.

Frank was less than forthright. Later, he explained that he had been in a crowded room full of supporters and that Barrett had asked if he had been in any incident in the last two weeks. April was long past and nothing had come of the episode. Perhaps Frank assumed or hoped it had been forgotten.

Barrett referred the matter to the attorney general's office for clarification, and suddenly a tidal wave of sensational media attention erupted. Where previously there had been no devastating publicity, the drinking incident now became widely and colourfully exploited. Rumours abounded. Barrett made appointments for Frank to discuss the situation with him in his office on July 20 and 27, but Frank did not return from his tour of Atlin to meet with his party leader.

No details between the two men were discussed face to face until the morning of July 31 when Frank met the premier in his office. Barrett was angry and gave Calder the opportunity to resign but Frank refused. It resulted in Barrett firing Calder from his cabinet post. To the press, Barrett announced only that he had "lost confidence in Calder." At least one columnist speculated that it may have been over the drinking incident but other reasons that were never cited were possible.[9] In hindsight, it seems doubtful that Barrett would have considered the drinking incident sufficient reason for firing Frank. If he had, he would not have waited three months to do so. When challenged, Barrett said he had not heard of the episode until July 4.

Iain Hunter, a reporter for the *Victoria Times* Ottawa Bureau, obviously believed that the situation involved far more than met the eye: "The strained relations between Ottawa and Victoria over Indian claims in the province was one of the factors leading up to the dismissal of Frank Calder from the BC cabinet July 31, it has been learned. Premier Dave Barrett fired the Nisga'a hereditary chief as minister without portfolio for what the premier described as Calder's failure to be 'forthright' about an incident involving a woman who was charged with impaired driving in Victoria last April. Barrett stated that he had lost confidence in his minister. But it appears that the incident was only the last of a series of actions by Calder, which made his position inside the NDP cabinet in Victoria untenable. While the final cause of his dismissal involved the personal affairs of the minister, the deeper differences between Calder and the rest of Barrett's cabinet was political, involving Indian Affairs. According to sources within Barrett's party, Calder was working too closely with the federal Liberals in seeking settlement of the Nisga'a land claims in BC."[10]

At the time, land claim negotiations were very much in the forefront of the Nisga'a agenda, and indeed for all First Nations people. The federal minister of Indian Affairs had publicly announced in parliament that they should begin. Frank knew there was federal support for the issue, and he may have become exceedingly tenacious in the provincial cabinet about beginning the restitution process. Whether or not his indignation over the provincial cabinet's ignoring Jean Chrétien on land claims was a factor in his firing, it is clear that he was given the opportunity to resign and refused. Barrett alleged Calder had lied to him and that he could not countenance such behaviour. Frank admitted that he had handled his dealings with Barrett poorly, but claimed he had not lied and emphasized that no charges were ever laid.

Frank's firing from cabinet embarrassed the Nisga'a Nation as well as the Calder family, and it was suggested that he resign as president of the Nisga'a Tribal Council. Much of the support he had won over the success of the Calder Case evaporated, and at that year's convention James Gosnell was elected president. Frank's long reign was over. After all, was not this the man who had repeatedly fought for full liquor privileges for Aboriginals? Wasn't he the only First Nations person who had risen to the post of cabinet minister? Had he not said that the white man should teach the Indian how to drink? If so, shouldn't he set an example, too? Devastated, Frank resigned as president. It was the pivotal turn in his political life. The stigma of his alleged wrong-doing became deeply embedded in the memories of many Canadians. The sensational "drunk driving incident," as it was termed, was even mentioned in a few obituaries written at the time of his death more than thirty years later. In the minds of many, it is the drinking that stands out and not the many, many improvements he achieved for northern BC. The summer of 1973 became the worst of times for his career. As a politician he never recovered.

In his final years Frank admitted to friends that he should have been a little more forthright when first questioned by Premier Barrett. However, in a column by Jim Hume on a different topic written many years later, a quote by Mahatma Gandhi was included. It seems appropriate to the situation and makes a telling final word. "Freedom is not worth having if it does not connote freedom to err. It passes my comprehension how human beings, be they ever so experienced and able, can delight in depriving other human beings of that right."[11] Jim Hume knew Frank well.

Four days later, Frank, no longer a cabinet member, was back in the legislature where the problem of other nations fishing in Canadian waters was once again brought to the fore. It was an issue on which Frank had advised for many years. Because Iceland had recently shot at some British fishers trespassing in their waters, it was suggested in the federal parliament that Canada should defend its waters in the same manner. Instead, the federal Conservatives and Liberals joined forces and produced a bill calling for a 200-mile limit for offshore fishing (320 kilometres). The following year there was to be an international "Law of the Sea" conference held in Chile, and the bill would put Canada in a strong position to have other nations recognize Canada's right to protect their fishers within this limit. In places where the continental shelf extended beyond 200 miles, the limit would be extended to the edge of the shelf. All parties supported the bill; the only argument in Ottawa seemed to be between the Conservatives and the Liberals as to who had suggested its introduction in the first place.[12] In the BC legislature Frank praised the way the issue had been handled.

The next important issue to occupy Frank was a clash between native fishermen and the United Fishermen and Allied Workers Union. The UFAWU wrote a letter to William King, the provincial minister of labour, asking that the UFAWU be named the sole bargaining unit for the industry. The Native Brotherhood of British Columbia wrote to the minister as well to request that traditional brotherhood hiring practices be respected. The Brotherhood, of course, expected support from Calder while the union expected support from the NDP. It was important because new labour legislation was being developed for the province, but Frank was not appointed to the committee. The letter from the Brotherhood claimed that the request by the UFAWU was an attempt to change the long-standing practice of joint negotiations. They claimed that the central hall practices, which were utilized by most unions, did not suit their traditional mode of hiring and would eliminate many Aboriginal people from the industry. The reply to both parties was that the matter would be studied. If Frank had been part of the negotiations might it have been possible that a compromise could have been negotiated? In the past he had had success. The matter was never fully resolved and even to the present day there are fierce arguments regarding fishing rights.

A long crusade that Frank had fought throughout his years in the house came to an end with the passage of Bill 93, "the Emergency Health Services Act." It resulted in Air Ambulance Service being established throughout the province. With its passage, Calder saw justice at last and was gratified that an inequitable hardship for people living in the north had at last been rectified. It had always been one of his most highly desired pieces of legislation, and one that had happened as a benefit of his own party holding power. Once the legislation passed, the service soon came into effect.[13]

A few months after the crushing incident of his firing, Frank met his future wife. He was dining out alone one evening in a Japanese restaurant where she was working as hostess. He had visited Japan and had liked the country and the people. As he watched the hostess move towards him bringing his order, he realized she was an attractive young woman, slight with a pretty face. Her graceful movements enchanted him. He smiled and tried to engage her in conversation, introducing himself and saying that he had been to Japan and liked the sound of the women's names. He asked for her name. Unlike in today's restaurants where the servers often tell the clients their names, she was extremely hesitant, replying in broken English that she could not tell him her name because he was a stranger.

Frank, however, was persistent and told her that if she told him her name he would promise never to forget it. Although still shy, she explained that her name would be hard to remember because it did not end in "ko" as did most Japanese women's names. Frank responded, saying,

"Please tell me anyway. It would make me very happy." And finally she told him that her name was Tamaki.

A week or so after, he went to see her again, but she had left the restaurant and he could not find her. Sometime later, by accident, he went into a coffee shop on Fort Street after getting his hair cut, and to his amazement found her working there. Immediately she said to him, "Do you remember my name? You promised you would never forget." He had to admit that he had forgotten, that she had been correct and that it was difficult for him to remember it. He suggested that they have dinner together one night soon, and she agreed. But then with little notice, Frank had to go to London on business and was delayed there. Once he was home again he made a point of going to see her and learned that, although she loved Victoria, she would be leaving shortly as she was here on a visa that would soon expire. He asked her the date and what flight she was planning to take. He thought about her often after that, and even though he did not know her very well, he sensed that he would miss her.

Impulsively, on the day she was leaving, he took a Pacific Stage Lines bus to Schwartz Bay that drove on board the BC ferry and proceeded to Vancouver airport. He knew Tamaki had to change planes there and would have a two-hour stop-over before boarding the next leg of her flight to Anchorage, the refuelling stop before Japan. He found her and awkwardly blurted out that she did not have to leave Canada, that she could marry him and stay in Canada. Tamaki was astounded. He knew by her face that he had made a terrible blunder. She replied heatedly, "I don't think so, but thank you for coming to see me off. Goodbye." She marched away. He thought he would never see her again.

After that there was nothing to do but travel back to Victoria. He felt despondent. He no longer had the usual tremendous amount of legislative work of previous years. He no longer held a cabinet post, and the court case was over. Life was not as vibrant or exciting as he had always found it. He had lost face with his party. He had lost face with the public, and he had lost face with his own people. Even the woman whose company he sought had angrily rejected him. It was a depressing time in his life. 1972 had started off so well; 1973 saw his successes turn to ashes.

CHAPTER 12

Frank Proposes

THE REMAINDER OF 1973 and the first part of 1974 was an empty period in Frank's life. In his fifties now, he had become thicker and stockier but retained his energetic ability for work even though he had less of it. He had always been busy with his career, but now that the land title case had been won and he was no longer a cabinet minister he had fewer responsibilities. There was less import to his daily activities; he began to feel bored and sensed a lack of meaning in his life.

Frank missed Tamaki after she went back to Japan and thought of her often. A bright spot for him was the day he received a postcard from her that she had mailed en route to Japan on her stopover in Anchorage. In it she apologized for being so abrupt and said it was nice of him to have come to the airport to see her off in Vancouver.

One evening in the fall of 1974, a happy grin spread over his face. He was out having dinner with friends and as he glanced around the room he noticed Tamaki sitting with a group a few tables away. Unexpectedly, but to his great delight, she had returned from Japan. They nodded to each other and he gave her a small wave. He left his seat and spoke to an acquaintance seated nearby, who he was sure would have her phone number. The very next morning he called her and apologized for his behaviour at the airport. He thanked her for the postcard she had sent and said he hoped they could see each other soon. He suggested that at long last they should have that dinner they had arranged so many months ago.

A few nights afterwards in the subdued lighting of a restaurant Frank particularly liked, he apologized for not having taken her to dinner before she left for Japan. He explained that he had been called away on business to London, England, that British Airways had gone on strike, and that he had been stranded there for five weeks. In turn, Tamaki explained that she'd had no way of knowing, that she had thought he had forgotten her and did not want to see her again. Although Tamaki was busy with other friends, Frank persisted and continued calling her, almost daily. She told him she was very unsure whether or not she wanted to develop a relationship with him. Sometimes when he had a date with her, she purposely made herself late. On one occasion she missed a dinner engagement entirely.

The next time they met he looked at her with a slight frown and said, "You are trying hard to be a very bad girl but I know you are not." Tamaki was stunned. He was exactly right. This man seemed to understand her — much better than her parents ever had. She reflected on what he had said and decided Frank deserved a chance. The months slipped by. They went out many times after that. One night over dinner, she told him the story of why she really had come to Canada. She described her story as follows:

"I was disgraced in Japan. To this day my sister will not speak to me. It all started during my last year at Keio University. I fell in love with a fellow student and was so happy. We met one afternoon at a dance when I had been asked to sing with the band. I love music and often sang at events. His name was Takashi and he was handsome, wealthy and fun. His parents owned a wholesale liquor business that serviced retail stores, bars and restaurants. He was attentive and very, very nice to me and we began spending more and more time together. I was impressed by how much he seemed to know, especially about the United States and found this very appealing. He was a very good dancer and we had many good times together. We fell in love with each other.

"Marriage in Japan is not at all like it is here. Children are expected to have their parents' permission. Often before giving permission they hire someone to investigate the other family; they want no surprises or secrets or hidden scandals that may embarrass them if they become in-laws. My parents forbade me to marry Takashi because an uncle of mine did not believe he was of good character.

"After graduation I unhappily returned home but a few weeks later a friend of Takashi's phoned me with a message from him. He said, 'Takashi begs you to meet him.' I was overjoyed and could hardly wait. We met in his apartment in Tokyo. He proposed and I accepted. Back home I told my mother the news and it upset her greatly. She was very, very angry. She said, 'If you marry Takashi you will never be a member of this family again. You will be disowned. We forbid it.'

"In tears I phoned Takashi and told him what she had said. He quickly replied, 'Pack all the belongings that you own, come to my apartment building, find my car and put your suitcase in it. I will look after you.' The very same day I did so. I knew it would mean giving up the chance of a good, arranged marriage. I knew it would demean and humiliate my parents but I was so in love that I didn't care. For a year Takashi and I lived together in his apartment. All the while, Takashi's mother worked hard so that we could be married. There is a custom in Japan that a son may not marry if he has a sister who is unmarried, and Takashi had a younger unmarried sister. His mother was a very nice woman and because Takashi wanted to marry, worked hard at arranging a good marriage for her daughter. After almost a year his sister was happily married and Takashi's mother arranged our marriage. Under the circumstances a traditional Japanese wedding was out of the question. My parents would have nothing to do with it. Takashi and I decided with his parents to be married in a small but lovely Christian church in Tokyo.

"Soon after the marriage I began to realize that Takashi had been spoiled from birth. His mother could deny him nothing. She bought us furniture that according to Japanese tradition my parents should have purchased but would not. At the same time she bought Takashi a red

Toyota, Mark II sports car that he coveted. He expected I would treat him the same way. I began to realize my marriage would be difficult.

"Ten months into our marriage Takashi did not return home one night. Upset, I phoned his mother but all she said was, "I am sorry but I cannot help you with this problem. Like some Japanese men, and because of our business I believe my son will always have mistresses.

"I could not accept it and he could not change. We grew further and further apart. The marriage became unbearable. One day my mother-in-law was visiting and advised me, 'You do not have a child; you can start a new life. I think it would be best.'

"I went home and my family welcomed me. Divorce proceedings started and they hired a good lawyer for me. Divorce is unacceptable in Japan and looked upon with dishonour. But that was not all. My sister Chiaki wanted to marry, and my divorce could easily cause the man's family to decide against marriage to her. My family needed me out of the way and decided that it would be best if I left Japan altogether. My father has a brother, Uncle Masujiro, who married a German woman, Aunt Maria. They live in Victoria. I agreed to go and visit them. I had a small inheritance and could easily afford it. My family soon made arrangements and purchased a one-way ticket to Victoria."[1]

Frank listened attentively and did not blame her behaviour in any way. He took her hand and quietly murmured, "I understand. It could not have been easy." As they got to know each other better Frank decided to take Tamaki to see his work place. It was a small unimpressive office in the legislative building with only one secretary that he shared with an officemate. It gave Tamaki no inkling that he was an elected member of the provincial government, and she certainly would never have guessed it from the appearance of his office. In Japan, elected members of any parliament always have large, plush offices, chauffeur-driven cars and several secretaries. Frank never boasted or tried to impress her in any way by saying that he had an important job, and it was a long time before she found out.

Another night when they were out walking, Frank told Tamaki the story of the old woman from Gingolx who had paddled all the way from the mouth of the Nass river to Greenville to foretell his birth. He told her it was why he had been adopted and came to have two families. He gave a small laugh, "Most people call it a myth and do not believe it."

Tamaki turned to him in amazement, "The Japanese believe there are fortune tellers. My mother took me to one when I was only about five years old. Japanese parents believe that it is useful to know what the future holds for their child. I remember that the soothsayer used a Chinese method of fortune telling by holding about two dozen thin, foot-long sticks in one hand. With the fingers of his other hand he divided the sticks here and there before spilling them out. It is a method that I believe is similar to tarot cards."

"And what did he say the future held for you?" Frank asked. She wasn't sure she wanted to tell him. Slowly she replied, "He told my mother that I would not live in Japan but would go to a far country and make my mark there." Frank grinned. "Canada is a far country." Tamaki said nothing, but Frank hoped that he would be the one to make the fortune come true.

Even while spending much time courting Tamaki, Frank never neglected the legislature. It would, however, never be the same for him after his disgrace. He was now a backbencher who had lost much of his prestige over being fired. *Hansard*, the official record of all legislative business, had started being kept in BC in 1970. It showed that Frank was always present and consistently voted, but that he did not rise and speak as often as he had in the past. Tamaki was the only bright spot in his life.

At this time the Canadian Prime Minister Pierre Elliott Trudeau had recently married Margaret Sinclair, the youngest daughter of James Sinclair, who had been federal minister of fisheries in a former Liberal cabinet. Frank had known the Sinclair family for many years, and Margaret when she was still a child. He knew she was almost as much younger than the prime minister as Tamaki was younger than he. Trudeau had been photographed wearing a leather jacket when he and Margaret were out walking together. Frank decided that style was important when courting a younger woman and bought a fashionable leather jacket, too.

Frank had fallen in love for the first time in his life. He began to bring Tamaki presents. Bouquets of silk flowers were one of his favourites. He considered them far superior to real roses because they did not fade. As the weather grew colder he presented her with a warm quilt so she would not be cold at night and bought her a record player so she would not be lonely. Chocolates and other gourmet items were frequent offerings.

In January Frank invited her to the traditional ball held at Government House, the lieutenant governor's official home, to celebrate the opening of the new session of the legislature. It was a grand affair held in the beautifully decorated ballroom of the imposing residence. Throughout the mansion there were huge bouquets of flowers, and an orchestra played in the background. The men were dressed in dinner jackets or formal military attire and the women in elegant evening gowns. Tamaki wore a long, red formal dress trimmed with gold that she has kept to this day. She had her hair done professionally, piled high on her head and wore gold high-heeled sandals.

Frank introduced Tamaki to Lieutenant Governor Walter Stewart Owen and Mrs. Owen and she met many other interesting people. Late in the evening after the speeches, introductions and dancing were over, a buffet was served. The long dining table was crammed with numerous delicacies and decorated with carved ice sculptures. Afterwards, Tamaki told Frank she had enjoyed every minute of the ball, but that she had not realized Frank was an elected member of the legislature, and that this was the reason why he had been invited.

Days later Frank proposed for the second time.

Tamaki slowly shook her head and explained that she wanted her freedom, that she liked her new lifestyle and did not want to marry. Frank responded by offering to give her all the freedom she wanted and told her that she could lead her life any way she wished. She thought about it and, as he watched her face, he added, "If you don't want to marry me I'll adopt you as my daughter. That way you still can stay in Canada." Tamaki laughed out loud and told him that she needed a few days to think it over. A big plus in Frank's favour was that Tamaki found him to be the kindest, most understanding man she had ever met.

Frank knew he was far too old for her, but even though she hadn't said yes, she had not said no either. He was now in his late fifties and she was more than twenty-five years younger. Still, he hoped that her answer would be "yes." During that week Tamaki seriously searched her soul.

She loved Victoria but wondered if she could live for the rest of her life in a country so vastly different from the one in which she had grown up. There was also the age difference; it would probably become a problem in the future. She thought back to her early childhood, dwelling on the astonishing prophecy the fortune teller had made. She thought again and again about what he had said. If she married Frank the prophecy would come true, and she would live in a country far away from Japan. It seemed as if it was meant to be. She loved Victoria and Frank was a kind, intelligent man. Finally, she made her decision. Frank waited a week, a week that seemed long to him, before she said with a smile, "Yes, I will marry you."

Frank was overjoyed and after giving her a big hug and kiss, laughed out loud with happiness. They were the most delightful words he could have heard. He told her, "I know I am too old for you but if Pierre can do it so can I." Suddenly life became the best of times again. The future looked bright and he resolved to find a useful purpose to serve.

Tamaki phoned her mother to tell her the news: "I have been proposed to by Frank Calder and I'm going to marry him. He is an Indian chief and. . . ." Tamaki never got any further before her mother replied angrily. "You are to come back to Japan on the very first flight out of Vancouver. Now!"

CHAPTER 13

Marriage

TAMAKI STAYED IN CANADA, married a Nisga'a chief, and never looked back. Frank made all the legal arrangements, and together they planned the wedding for the following month, February. He and Tamaki had grown up in very different societies. Their ages, the marriage rites of their people, their education and backgrounds were vastly divergent. By selecting a bride not of Canadian descent, Frank displayed as much rugged individualism in his private life as he had in his political life. He had waited a long time to marry and often had thought he never would. As always, he followed his heart and his deep inner feelings. To him the marriage felt right.

In the marriage ceremony they planned, Tamaki and Frank would defy the conventions of both their families. Tamaki did not have parental approval. She had been brought up in a society where rigid marriage traditions were enforced. Parents arranged suitable spouses for their children, and even though the wishes of the children were considered, parents made the ultimate decision. The decisions as to paying for the marriage costs, arranging the marriage ceremony and for establishing a home for the young couple were divided according to custom and shared by both families. Tamaki had defied the marriage tradition of her people before coming to Canada. By marrying Frank she would do so again.

Because he belonged to a family of Nisga'a chiefs, Frank had been expected to follow the tradition of choosing a bride from another family of the same class. The Calders, however, had brought Frank up believing in the Anglican rites of marriage and had never subscribed to those of the old Nisga'a tradition.

Nevertheless, even if deeply buried, some elements of Frank's ancient culture remained. An old manuscript typed in red ink and signed *Weinal'th*, meaning Big Black Fish, exists among Frank's belongings. The quality of the English is somewhat broken. Frank's sister, Dorothy, and brother, Phillip, believe that Frank typed it one or two years after he went to Co-qualeetza. He and all his siblings belonged to the Killer Whale clan, and at that time on the coast of British Columbia killer whales were commonly referred to as Big Black Fish. Today they are called by their scientific name of orcas and are a protected species. Part of the manuscript describes the marriage traditions of the Nisga'a (see appendix 4 for Frank's original text).

Here, in brief, is a summary of the traditional Nisga'a marriage customs in the pre-contact period, as Frank understood them:

There were two classes of Nisga'a; the common class to which most Nisga'a belonged and the upper class that consisted of the families of the chiefs of the four clans. In either class once a girl reached womanhood she was not allowed to go out at night unless her mother went with her. It was the Nisga'a way of preventing children from being born out of wedlock, at least in the period before they became Christian.

In the common class when a young man reached the age of twenty, the man's father and uncles and all the clan would choose the right girl for him. Then the groom-to-be would give his future mother-in-law a valuable present. The first time he gave the gift she always returned it but if the man's family were serious about the marriage he would give it a second time. When the girl's mother accepted the gift her father would set a date for the wedding to take place in a year's time.

After this the young man moved from his home to live with and work for his future father-in-law. During this year he could not even take his wife-to-be out for a walk. She in turn was forbidden to go near him. When the wedding took place, a great feast or wedding breakfast was held for the entire village. From then on the couple lived together as man and wife but they continued to live in the house of the wife's parents and he continued to work for his father-in-law until he had enough savings for the couple to move out on their own.

A high-class wedding when a future chief married a princess was somewhat different. It was an event that provided entertainment for the whole village. The bride would stand in the doorway of her home dressed in her wedding clothes with her uncle by her side and a pantomime ensued. Her entire clan stood behind her ready for mock battle. Also ready for battle the groom's clan stood in front of him. The groom's clan then tried to capture the girl while the bride's family tried to stop them. Everyone in the village watched the show with much laughter. It was all in fun and always ended with the groom's family capturing the bride. Afterwards the entire village was invited to a great feast.

In spite of their cultural differences, on February 26, 1975, Frank and Tamaki exchanged vows. It was just over a month after the ball at Government House. It would be a wedding that neither of them could ever have imagined during their years growing up. For Tamaki it began early Wednesday morning when she dressed carefully in her white silk kimono with much embroidery on it. The traditional Japanese wedding kimono of rich, red brocade decorated with much gold was not available to her, and this was the best she owned. At the appointed time she took a taxi to Fort Street where Frank had asked her to meet him. There he escorted her inside to the marriage commissioner's office where a justice of the peace was waiting. Leo Nimsick, the minister of Highways, and Mrs. Nimsick were waiting along with Mary Christiansen, Frank's secretary. They had come to witness the couple's marriage vows. After the brief ceremony, everyone wished the newlyweds a long and happy life together.

From there the Nimsicks drove Frank and Tamaki to the legislative buildings. Frank and Leo took their seats in the house, and Mrs. Nimsick guided Tamaki to the Public Gallery. At last, Frank's bride experienced the full impact of her new husband's being an elected member of

Frank and Tamaki in her Japanese kimono, shortly after their
wedding in Victoria, February 26, 1975. Courtesy *Times Colonist*.

the legislature and realized he had enjoyed an impressive career. Shortly,
the Hon. Leo Nimsick rose and was recognized by the Speaker.

"Mr. Speaker and Members of the Legislature, I've got a very pleasant
duty to perform to-day and a surprising introduction to make to the
house. Back in 1949 when I first entered the House, there were quite a

number of members here but today there are only two of us who came in at that time, Frank Calder and myself. At that time he was classified as the baby of the House. I've known Frank for these 26 years. I've worked with him. At times I've tried to match him up, but Frank was very particular, and went on for 26 years without being caught. (Laughter.)

"But a few years ago he made a trip to Japan. Now I don't know why he made that trip to Japan, or what happened. But a short time ago a visitor from Japan was here and the other day I was introduced to the surprise; I was asked to be witness, along with Mary Christiansen and my wife, at a very enjoyable ceremony. "I would like to introduce Mrs. Frank Calder to you today."[1]

All the members thumped their desks and clapped enthusiastically as they cheered their good wishes and looked upwards towards the gallery where Tamaki was seated. Frank sat with a big grin on his face. Nimsick then concluded, "I am sure that response means you wish them the very best for the future. Mrs. Calder's name happens to be 'Tami.' I hope that we make her a pleasant welcome to British Columbia."[2]

A few minutes later, a messenger arrived in the gallery with a note from Frank asking Tamaki to meet him at the Golden Arch of the legislative building. She had no idea where the Golden Arch was located, but Mrs. Nimsick knew exactly and guided her there. Frank emerged from the house almost immediately and stood at her elbow. A photographer appeared and the flash bulb of his camera flashed repeatedly sending small, black dots dancing in front of their eyes. Several shots were taken. To their surprise, the next morning one of the photographs appeared on the front page of the *Victoria Colonist*.

Their honeymoon would have to be delayed. The legislature was still in session and Frank had work to do. He served on various committees and was always conscientious about doing the best he could for his constituents. The NDP party was in power, which was favourable for much of the legislation he hoped would be passed. The negotiations to settle land claims continued to be extremely important to him, but they were receiving no support whatsoever. No member on either side of the house was anxious to tackle the problem.

Frank and his bride settled into the little house on the Gorge in Victoria that Frank had purchased several years previously. A few weeks later, Tamaki was surprised when she discovered that her husband had no money saved. She knew he had very high expenses because of travel to his distant riding, but her father, a prominent Japanese banker, had taught her about the importance of keeping and balancing a budget. Both he and Tamaki's mother had always been careful with money and had kept good accounts. Together the newly married couple decided that it would be best if Tamaki managed the family finances, which is not an uncommon practice for Japanese wives. She was determined to save and economize on everything. Frank sometimes joked to people, "I'm the only MLA who has to brown bag it to work," but he was secretly proud of her.

Three months later the legislature adjourned and they travelled north for a very different marriage ceremony. It was neither Nisga'a nor Japanese but a traditional Anglican ceremony that meant a great deal to Frank. He had graduated from the Anglican Theological College at the University of British Columbia and had been educated by Anglican missionaries.

To reach the riding they flew first to Terrace where a car and driver took them more than sixty miles over gravel roads to the shore of the Nass River. There, in a small boat, they crossed to the village of Greenville. Tamaki had never experienced any travel like it or even glimpsed the Canadian wilderness before. She found it hard to believe there was any place on earth so solitary and devoid of conveniences. For the two hours it took to drive from Terrace to Greenville they did not pass a single café, store or gas station. She had never imagined any area on earth could be as isolated as this.

On arrival in Greenville they were greeted by Frank's sister Bertha and taken to her comfortable house. Tamaki was surprised at how immaculate and well furnished it was. A beautiful crystal chandelier was hanging in the hallway and a piano figured prominently in the living room. To her, like many other people, she believed "Indian" meant "primitive," and here in the middle of Canada's wilderness she discovered that it was not so.

There was a second surprise when Bertha took her to the bedroom she and Frank were to share and showed her a lovely white wedding dress that she and her family had sewn for her wedding. It was hanging, perfectly pressed and waiting. To everyone's utter amazement it was an excellent fit and Tamaki considered the sewing outstanding. Before the wedding Frank had started to call her "Tami," and soon she became known to all Frank's relatives as Auntie Tami. It is what Frank's family calls her to this day.

They were married for the second time in Greenville's small white church that had been built to replace a beautiful wooden structure with stained glass windows. The original church had taken forty years to build, but after the tremendous effort and care that had gone into its construction, it had unfortunately burned to the ground in 1962. None of its contents were saved, including an exquisitely carved baptismal font and holy table.

The Anglican ceremony was on May 24, 1975, to the strains of the "Wedding March" echoing from a handsome organ that years ago had been transported with great difficulty to the distant church. A large reception in the Nisga'a Hall followed. The banquet food was lavish and

Frank and Tamaki after their Anglican wedding in Greenville.
Tamaki is wearing the wedding dress Frank's sisters made for her.

consisted of traditional smoked seal, salmon, oolichan and kelp, along with many kinds of western food. Of course, there was a huge wedding cake ceremoniously cut by the bride and groom that provided dessert for everyone.

Afterwards, the couple left for their delayed honeymoon in Hawaii. Gordon Gibson, well known in the lumber industry in British Columbia and a Liberal who had been a fellow MLA of Frank's, gave them a wonderful wedding present. It was the use of a cottage in Maui Lu, the resort his family owned on the island of Maui. The cottage was perched on a beautiful sand beach, and Tamaki particularly remembers the grapefruit tree from which she picked fresh fruit for their breakfasts.

One very hot day, they went into town to do some shopping. When they were finished, they stood on the sidewalk and looked at each other wondering how they were ever going to get everything back to Maui Lu. There was not a taxi in sight. A very kind Portuguese gentleman standing nearby saw their dilemma, came over and offered to help. He drove them home in his own car. On the way to Maui Lu he told them that he was married to a native Hawaiian woman, and he was interested to learn that Frank was Aboriginal too. He was fascinated when he heard that Frank was the man who had played such an important part in the Canadian Supreme Court decision that had initiated recognition of Aboriginal land title. He knew of the decision and very much wanted Frank to talk to his wife.

The next day he picked them up in his car and took them to his home where they met his Hawaiian wife and three children. His daughter danced traditional Hawaiian dances for them, and they had a very pleasant day. Before they left, a meeting was arranged between native Hawaiians and Frank to discuss land claims. The decision in the Calder Case had far-reaching effects everywhere, and particularly for Hawaiians because of their British background. The native people of Hawaii believed a first-hand account would be useful to them. Frank was pleased to provide as much information as possible in a short time. After the meetings, the newlyweds played golf, swam and sunbathed for a week and then flew to Oahu for a second week before flying back to Victoria to continue their busy life.

One of the changes Tamaki made in their lives was the purchase of a car. Frank had never owned a car. He did not want to drive and was not interested in obtaining a driver's license. Tamaki insisted she would do the driving. She told him how much easier life would be for him when she could drive him everywhere. Finally they purchased a second-hand Ford Colt. It gave Tamaki a great sense of independence, and it proved to be an economical decision because earlier they had spent a good deal of Frank's income on taxis. As well as the convenience of having their own transportation, Frank discovered it was a great time saver.

A few months later they flew to Prince Rupert for a basketball tournament in which Nisga'a teams were competing. Frank was invited because he had always been a strong supporter of Aboriginal sports, and he was asked to speak to the gathering once the competition was over. In the audience the four Nisga'a chiefs of the clans were seated: the Killer Whale, the Wolf, the Frog and the Eagle. Even though they had been married for seven months Tamaki had never been formally initiated into the Nisga'a Nation. Two of the four clans were vying for her to become a member of their circle, the Wolf clan and the Eagle clan. When the tournament ended and Frank finished his speech, the chief of one of the clans stood. It was Bill McKay, of the Wolf Clan. He was the first to stand and, according to tradition, the first to stand had the right to claim. Tamaki would be initiated into the Wolf Clan.

The next September as the summer weather drew to a close, Frank and Tamaki travelled north once more. This time it was for his annual tour of the vast riding of Atlin. In the Nisga'a community hall in Greenville where their wedding reception had been held, Tamaki was inducted as a Nisga'a princess. The name bestowed on her was Mithlkum Belis, which means "shining star." She was given traditional regalia, a cape and a headband indicating that she was indeed a princess. She didn't understand a single word of the ceremony because it was entirely in Nisga'a but felt truly honoured. Now she had become a member of the Wolf clan, Frank typed the oral history of the clan handed down from generation to generation, as it had been told to him by his birth father Job Clark. Both he and his father thought it might be useful when land claim compensation began.

Frank on tour in his riding of Atlin, camping
with his wife Tammy, 1975.

Frank and Tammy visiting a gold sluice with an unknown gold
prospector while on tour in Atlin.

Tamaki had never lived in a wilderness area and certainly had never camped. It was an entirely new experience for her. As the tour progressed, they occasionally had to sleep in a tent. There was no public transportation and they did not have a four-wheel-drive vehicle. The only solution was to hitch rides any way they could. The department of highways was helpful, road crews sometimes took them from place to place, and occasionally mining camp personnel would drive them. Once they travelled by boat.

The weather was glorious, sunny and warm, and everywhere people were very friendly. In Stewart the mayor greeted them, and from there they travelled to the Dease Lake District. In an area around the lake called Etom Donajonin, Frank told Tamaki an old legend of how a broken-hearted lover had jumped into Dease Lake and drowned himself.

One night while camping, a native couple in a tent next to them was smoking salmon. They were Mr. and Mrs. Ezacha, who had eighteen children. In the morning Mrs. Ezacha cooked pancakes and sausages and invited them for breakfast. The Japanese do not eat sweets in the morning and never meats as fatty as sausage. Tamaki was wondering if she could eat enough to be polite until she tried it and pronounced it "truly delicious." The trip to Atlin turned out to be a wonderful adventure as well as a good public relations trip for Frank.

The next month in October they attended the Annual Nisga'a Convention in Greenville. (The name had been changed from "Tribal Council" to "Convention" after the Calder Case.) Autumn can be a stunning season in the north when the air is sharp and the fall colours brilliant against the evergreens thick with needles. Frank was no longer president of the convention but supported the new president, James Gosnell, a long-time member of the Nisga'a council. The convention's agenda was full with many long-time items still unresolved and new problems arising around them. Fishing rights, highways, lack of services and access to health care as always were under discussion. A new issue now that the Calder Case had been settled was the negotiation for recompense of land claims. It was a momentous issue, and one that every Nisga'a was looking forward to having resolved. Many considered that Frank was in a position to have negotiations for compensation begin and were increasingly unhappy he had not yet even managed to get them started.

The Ezacha family with their eighteen children. Mrs. Ezacha cooked pancakes and
sausages for Frank and Tamaki when they were on tour in Atlin.

Tamaki coming out of a
tent while on tour in
Atlin. She had never
slept in a tent before.

During a break in the long agenda, a delegate rushed up to Frank and urgently asked, "Did you know that Premier Barrett has called an election?" Frank looked dumbfounded. The man continued, "I was listening to the radio and just heard that an election has been called for December."

Frank was flabbergasted. When he had left Victoria he did not have a hint an election was anywhere in the offing. The NDP were only three years into their mandate and previously had criticized as wasteful the Social Credit practice of calling elections every three years. Still, Dave Barrett had noted that the practice had been successful for his predecessor and now he was in power had obviously decided to follow his example.

On hearing the news, Frank immediately contacted his Victoria office. The news became more and more unbelievable. He was told that a nomination meeting had already been held for the riding of Atlin, and that another NDP candidate, Gordon Steidel, had been selected to run in Frank's stead. Frank had not even been informed a nomination meeting was taking place. He was one of the longest-standing NDP members and a former cabinet minister for the party and had not heard a whisper that any of these proceedings were taking place. Hastily, Frank and Tamaki returned to Victoria.

As they travelled south, Frank was in distress and saw his entire career dissolving in shambles. He believed his misdemeanor when he was caught with a woman and alcohol in the car might have been used as the grounds to oust him. Firing from cabinet had been bad enough but this was hard to believe. He had faithfully served the riding of Atlin and represented the NDP for well over twenty-three years and, without the slightest hint to him, he had been unceremoniously dumped.

Frank was in a quandary but did not cross the floor of the legislature, and in any case could not do so because the house was not in session. However, without a riding to run in he had to give serious consideration to his future. In cases of this nature it is common for the member to run as an independent. However, both the Liberal and Social Credit parties contacted him informally, which led to a great deal of thought on his part.

The consequences of speaking against one's party's policies are so devastating that it is rare for any politician to be strong enough to do so. Trying to make up his mind what to do, Calder recalled the case of Winston Churchill, a leader he greatly admired. No less a man than Churchill had done the same when he attacked the defence policy of his government, believing that money should not be spent on ships and guns but on social programs.[3] In May 1904 he was forced to resign from the Conservative party. Moreover, in the period between the First and Second World Wars Churchill was discredited and vilified by friends and opponents alike when he reversed his policy and supported the military. Frank realized he was now paying a price for the stances he had taken against the NDP — just as Churchill had paid a price.

In considering his choice between the Liberal and the Social Credit parties, Frank recognized that, after losing the last provincial election, the Social Credit party had made a strong effort to reassert itself. The retirement of long-time Premier WAC Bennett had left the organization without an obvious choice for a new leader, but party insiders had finally persuaded his son Bill Bennett to take his father's place. Although he was young and good looking, he lacked the charisma his father had exuded. Nevertheless, he had grown up in a political household and understood politics well. He was dedicated to British Columbia and with his strong business background was determined to steer the province to an improved financial position.

After a few days of thought Frank decided to join the renewed Social Credit Party. They were delighted to hear from him and shortly arranged a meeting for him with their campaign committee. It took place in the Harbour Towers Hotel in downtown Victoria. When he arrived with Tamaki, they were greeted with smiles and welcomed warmly. The issue of Frank's rude unseating by the NDP was discussed. It was assumed the main reasons were that he had embarrassed his party by his outspokenness about the dearth of First Nations membership in unions and that he had been too insistent on beginning land claim negotiations. He had defied his party by fighting the unpopular Calder Case in the first place and the fact that the federal government had sided with him on land claims had only increased their hostility towards him. It had placed the NDP in a very awkward position. If they refused to begin land claim negotiations they could be accused of ignoring an all-party vote in the federal parliament, and if they began negotiations they could lose much support from the electorate. The general public viewed land claims in British Columbia with great suspicion.

After a thorough discussion, matters were settled and Frank was invited to run in the riding of Atlin as a Social Credit candidate. As they were leaving, the last words the campaign manager spoke were, "Thank you for coming to our party." A few days later, Bill Bennett formally welcomed him, and the photograph of him doing so appeared in numerous newspapers throughout BC.

On December 11, 1975, the election was held and Frank won easily in Atlin with 984 votes to Gordon Steidel's 497. The Social Credit party under Bill Bennett gained a strong majority and won thirty-five seats, to only eighteen by the NDP. The province was in debt and the general public believed that the NDP had not handled finances prudently. The Socreds claimed that the NDP had behaved "like kids let loose in a candy store." Frank may have felt some uneasiness to see his old party lose power, but he was pleased that he had chosen the party that had won power. It was always easier to pass legislation if one belonged to the party that governed.

At the next Social Credit convention the old premier, WAC Bennett, stopped Frank in the hall, shook his hand and said, "I always knew you would come to us one day. I knew it! I knew it!"

CHAPTER 14

The Legislature, 1976–1979

IMMEDIATELY AFTER THE election campaign, the Calders flew to Japan. Frank had never met Tamaki's family but knew they were dismayed that their daughter had married an "Indian," which from their point of view meant a "primitive." Before their marriage, Tamaki had suggested that Frank write a letter to her father to introduce himself and to let him know that his daughter had married an educated man. Now Tamaki wanted all her family to know her husband and see for themselves who he was. As well, Tamaki thought if Frank learned about her family and background he would understand her better. She had been to his land and now he would come to hers.

Although the visit was a success, it also had a sad side because when they arrived they discovered that Tamaki's father was ill in the hospital with cancer. Even though he was very weak, her father rose from his bed and bowed to his son-in-law when Frank was introduced. He and Frank spoke together for some time and seemed to like each other. Tamaki's mother was also polite to Frank. All her life she would wish that her daughter had married someone else, but at this point she seemed to accept her son-in-law. In return, Frank made every effort to please her and continued to do so until her death many years later.

While they were in Japan, a weekly woman's magazine, *Josei Jishin*, interviewed Tamaki and wrote about her life in Victoria. This resulted in the one unfortunate incident of their visit. Tamaki's sister Chiaki had married while Tamaki was away and had never told her mother-in-law about her sister's marriage or that her husband was an Indian. When Chiaki's mother-in-law came across the article, she was very annoyed with her daughter-in-law because she knew the marriage to Frank would create much gossip among her friends. As a result, Chiaki was furious with her sister. It created a rift between Chiaki and Tamaki that never fully healed, but aside from this issue, the Koshibe family appeared to accept Frank well.

The visit was short and took place over the Christmas holidays, which are celebrated in Japan even though it is not a Christian country. Because the celebration of the New Year is much more important in Japan, Frank and Tamaki stayed for it but once it was over flew home to Victoria. After they left, Tamaki's father returned home for a short while because he did not like the hospital. His wife kept her belief alive that he was improving, but unfortunately that was not the case. The New Year's celebration was the last time Tamaki ever spoke with him. She was always pleased that he and Frank had met and that they had liked and respected each other.

In January of 1976 the thirty-first session of the legislature of British Columbia was sworn in. Frank was back in the legislature, and a new experience awaited him. He was a member of a different party, Social Credit, the party that had been his opposition for many years. No longer was he a long-standing party member but instead a neophyte. After reviewing the province's finances, the new government concluded that British Columbia was heavily in debt. Premier Bill Bennett, the new leader, had a strong business background and was determined to correct the problem. He began by instituting an austerity program. He cancelled the traditional ball held at Government House to celebrate the start of a new legislative session and did away with the outdoor lighting that trimmed the outline of the legislative buildings at night. He made cuts in all areas of government spending. The unions became angry and claimed that the lower level of government services was causing hardship. Austerity at any time is unpopular.

Frank's concern as always was for the people of his riding. Now that it was recognized that Aboriginal people had held land title before the Europeans arrived, and the federal government was willing to negotiate claims, he pressed hard to have the province begin the process. However, the government of the day considered that other matters, especially finances, were far more pressing.

Six months later, in June, the newly married couple received the news that Tamaki's father was dying. Immediately, they decided that Tamaki should fly to Japan and visit him in hospital. Frank would be unable to accompany her because of his legislative duties. When she arrived, Tamaki found he could not speak and she never knew if he understood what she said or not. She stayed for the funeral and comforted her mother as best she could. Tamaki returned home to Victoria without realizing how deeply her father's death had affected her mother. In Japan it is customary for guests to give money at funerals, and during a phone call her mother told Tamaki that she was unable to count the funeral money properly. She said that every time she did so she got a different total. Because her mother had always been good with accounts, Tamaki knew something was seriously wrong. She flew to Japan, straightened out the accounts, and with Frank's blessing brought her mother back to Canada to visit them.

In Victoria, her mother remained depressed. Frank and Tamaki decided that a holiday might help to relieve her misery. As Frank was busy Tamaki took her to Banff and Lake Louise on the train. The grandeur of the towering mountains amazed her mother. She had never seen anything like them and began to take an interest in the magnificence all around her. One day she claimed, "The mountains have opened up the beauty of the world to me and taught me that I should not feel sorry for myself." She decided that she liked Canada very much, and the trip finally managed to relieve her depression. Two years later Frank helped Mrs. Koshibe become a landed immigrant, and she moved permanently to Victoria.

In the spring of 1977 a prominent Japanese television studio, Tokyo

Broadcasting System (TBS), contacted Tamaki with a request to make a film that would feature both her and her chieftain husband, Frank. They had heard that a Japanese woman who was a graduate of Keio University, regarded as the top private university in Japan, had married an Indian chief. They considered it such an amazing story they believed it should be filmed. They decided to title the presentation, *Keio Woman Graduate Marries Indian Chief*.[1]

Six months later, a television crew arrived in Victoria and immediately flew to the Nisga'a reserve to shoot the raising of a totem pole. The studio believed such a unique ceremony would be of great interest to their audience and would illustrate well the culture in which Frank had grown up. The raising of a totem, entirely without machinery, is an amazing sight involving over one hundred men and many hours of hard labour. During some stages it can be dangerous. The totem they filmed was raised in New Aiyanish on the Nass for a highly symbolic purpose. It had been carved by Eli Gosnell to represent the unity of the entire Nisga'a Nation.[2] Gosnell had carved it using ten major symbols including those of the four clans, the Killer Whale, the Frog, the Wolf and the Eagle. At the very top he had carved a rainbow that represented the dawning of a new era of unity for the Nisga'a people. There were over two thousand members who lived in the Nass Valley and two thousand who lived elsewhere but kept in close contact with the Nisga'a. The totem would symbolize their affinity.[3] It was a very special event to be caught on film. (The accompanying sketch of the Nisga'a Unity Pole is courtesy of Leith Harper.)

Back in Victoria the Calders' life style was the main focus of the TBS crew. They shot film of the Calders' house on the Gorge and also the house Tamaki had boarded in before she married Frank. TBS then went to Beacon Hill Park and filmed the couple out walking. They also included footage of the legislature and other points of interest. Frank found the filming experience an interesting diversion from the legislative debates. Later, to finish the movie, TBS flew them both to Japan for ten days. The company arranged with the airline that, when the plane landed, the Calders would be the first to deplane at Haneda Airport, the Tokyo airport before Narita was built. They were requested to wear full Indian regalia as they descended. A crowd awaited their arrival and proved extremely curious about them as they walked towards the terminal.

At their hotel, the director asked Frank what sights he most wanted to see in Japan, as they wanted to make arrangements for filming ahead of time. He chose Kyoto, the ancient capital of Japan. There, as well as the golden palace, he wanted to see the famous Maiko, young girls in training to become dancers. Another city he asked to visit was Hiroshima. He also expressed special interest in visiting the Museum of Aboriginal People in Osaka. Frank knew that Japan had had an Aboriginal population just like many other countries all over the world: the Maori in New Zealand, the Aborigines in Australia and the Hill People in the triangle where Thailand, Myanmar and Laos meet.

The Museum of Aboriginal People did not disappoint Frank. He knew before his visit that in Japan the Aboriginal people were called Ainu and he was interested to learn more about their history. He found

Frank and Tamaki in Hiroshima, Japan, where they toured at the request of the Tokyo Broadcasting System, 1977.

the museum had documented their past well. The Ainu had settled in the Japanese archipelago about ten thousand years ago. They were Animists, a belief that ascribes souls to all natural objects: humans, animals and plants. They wore simple robes called *attush* spun from the inner bark of the elm tree and tied with a cord. The men tended to be proud of their hair and wore moustaches and full beards. Like the women, they did not let their hair grow in length beyond their neck. They spoke a distinct language unrelated to any other and had a number of different dialects. They had no written language and because of this, in common with most other Aboriginal peoples including the Nisga'a, they had a great tradition of storytelling.

Frank found a parallel between the history of the Ainu and that of his own people, except that in Japan the intrusion of a stronger culture had taken place much earlier. The Yayoi or Japanese people had come to the islands some twenty-five hundred years ago and begun to settle among the Ainu. Like the Europeans in North America, the Japanese soon became the dominant culture. Slowly they displaced the Aboriginals who retreated north to the Island of Hokkaido and south to the Island of Ryukyu. Over the years there were skirmishes between the Ainu and the sovereign Japanese but for the most part the Ainu retreated peacefully. The diseases of smallpox and measles introduced by the Yayoi greatly reduced their numbers just as they had to the native populations in North America when introduced by the Europeans.

Assimilation had been the official Japanese government policy toward the Ainu. This was accomplished by outlawing their language and giving them plots of land to farm. Inter-marriage had been encouraged. Frank discovered that the result of Japanese policies was that twenty-five hundred years later, the Ainu could hardly be distinguished from the general population. Among the Ainu, moreover, feelings of inferiority remained in their descendants, and many try to hide their Aboriginal ancestry because of prejudice against it as being primitive compared to Japanese culture. Frank learned that there were no true Ainu communities in Japan, and their culture has been preserved only through crafts that command high prices.[4]

Frank was surprised to find that not only did the museum illustrate

Frank and Tamaki at the Folklore Museum in Japan where a
Nisga'a totem and blanket were displayed, 1977.

the Ainu traditions but those of many other Aboriginal people around the
world. The collection was extensive. Along with artifacts from many
societies he was amazed to find that it even displayed an authentic
Nisga'a blanket. He recognized it immediately.

Frank received a great deal of publicity throughout the visit. In the
national newspaper *Mainichi*, a regular column titled "The Man" was
published daily. One day that week it was devoted to Frank and explained
who he was, where he had come from and what he had accomplished. A
daily television program titled *Let Us Meet at Three O'Clock* screened a
one-hour special about the couple to be shown the following Friday. On
the Monday, Tuesday, Wednesday and Thursday before the presentation
the last ten minutes of every program were devoted to the activities they
had engaged in that day. It was used as advertising to entice people to
watch on Friday.

Frank wanted to see the emperor but that was not possible, and so a
visit to the Diet, the Japanese Parliament, was arranged instead. Again
they were requested to attend in full native regalia. At the door of the

chamber Frank was told he could not bring his talking stick inside because nothing dangerous was allowed. Frank did not accept this and insisted that he would not be a chief without his stick, and so the rule was relaxed. After the Diet they were taken to the office of Mr. Ohira, the minister of Foreign Affairs. As they entered they saw half a dozen men in attendance, who were his assistants. When Mr. Ohira entered they all immediately stood at attention. When in turn each was introduced to them, each man bowed and said, "Nice to meet you." Frank and Mr. Ohira exchanged greetings and comments about Japan. As they were leaving, Tamaki said to the minister, "When you become prime minister please come to Canada and visit us." His assistants were visibly shocked that she would speak to such an important man and extend an invitation. In Japan, such invitations are issued only through diplomatic channels. She was just trying to be friendly but perhaps she had been away too long.

They returned to Victoria and Frank continued with his duties as MLA. He presented a proposal for a new road to be constructed between Terrace and the villages on the Nass using a route that would avoid the need for additional bridges. This would save costs. He also pushed for jobs for Aboriginal people on the construction of it. Once again, he pressed for land claim negotiations to begin, but again he was unsuccessful.

The autumn of 1977 was a very busy time for the Calders. From October 14 to 19, Canada received an historic visit from Queen Elizabeth and Prince Philip. The Queen was travelling to many countries throughout the world to mark her Silver Jubilee, the twenty-fifth year of her ascension to the throne. Frank, because of his long-standing membership in the legislature and other accomplishments, was invited to Ottawa to meet her. Tamaki, as his wife, would attend with him. The visit coincided with the formal opening of the parliamentary session in Ottawa. Queen Elizabeth gave the speech from the throne that ordinarily would have been read in her absence by her Canadian representative, Governor General Jules Léger.

Frank and Tamaki along with many others sat silently in their seats and listened to her opening speech before moving to a very large room for a reception that was held in her honour. The room was huge and the number of people large, as the Queen slowly made her way around the perimeter, greeting each dignitary in turn. She stopped in front of Frank, took his hand and smiled, "We have met before." Frank nodded and smiled widely in return. "Yes, in 1971 to celebrate British Columbia's centennial and before that when you were still a princess." She nodded. "Yes, I remember you." She looked directly at Tamaki standing beside Frank. Tamaki curtsied before the Queen moved on, but neither one said anything. Frank wondered if, because of her extensive travels, she recognized that the woman standing beside him was Japanese and found it odd. When she was a short distance away the Queen looked back at Tamaki with a puzzled look on her face. After the ceremony, they did not linger in Ottawa because Frank had to return to work. On the flight home, however, they happily reminisced about their enjoyable experience. It was one they would always remember.

When the next session of the legislature adjourned, Tamaki decided that Frank needed a holiday. Although he had travelled to London, Tokyo and Sydney on government business, he said to Tamaki: "Except for our honeymoon, I have never had a real holiday. I can't afford one."

"Yes, you can," she replied. "There is money I have saved and we can pay for it with that." A few weeks later they flew to London. From there they took a bus tour to York and Edinburgh and along the way stopped to see the sights. Once back in London they spent a few days there before flying to France. There they booked another bus trip, this time a whirlwind tour of the countries of Switzerland, Austria, Italy and the Netherlands. Then it was back to London for their return flight home. In that short time they saw a great many places. Frank found it wonderful to travel without a briefcase full of work following him. They wished it could last longer but, regardless, they considered it worthwhile. They viewed much Gothic style architecture that Tamaki had never seen before and historic cathedrals that were of particular interest to Frank because of his religious training.

Fall was the time of the Nisga'a Convention, the time when Frank took his annual tour of his riding. Again he left Victoria with Tamaki, flew to Terrace and then drove to the riding of Atlin. As they toured from place to place, they found the atmosphere very different from what it had been during their last visit. The school principals, teachers and others were unfriendly and did not give Frank the welcome he had always experienced on previous visits.

Everywhere they went there were questions about starting negotiations for land claims. Frank had been doing his best but the government of the day was completely enmeshed in questions of the economy. The unemployment rate was high, the forest industry on which the province depended was in a downturn, and the unions were angry. None of this meant anything to the Nisga'a. They had contributed large sums of money to support three court cases. They had won, and now wanted to see some recompense in return. They felt land negotiations should have started and that compensation for past wrongs was long past due. Because he was a member of the legislature, Frank, they believed was in the best position to begin the process, and they blamed him for the delay. He tried to explain that he was doing everything he could.

When they arrived back in Victoria, Frank found the political climate in the province had deteriorated even further. The economy was mired in "stagflation," and some economists were predicting it would become even worse. There seemed to be no easy solutions. The year finally dragged to an end with little change. In the new year, government revenues continued to fall, triggering more cutbacks. The government steadily lost popularity. When Bill Bennett saw that the economic situation was unlikely to improve in the near future, he decided to act. Tamaki happened to be visiting the legislature about this time and was amazed to see Socred MLA Don Phillips striding down the hall of the legislature in great excitement calling out: "There's going to be an election! There's going to be an election!" Bennett set the date for May 10, 1979. Frank did not think that it was a wise decision, but most members supported it. After the announcement, he told Tamaki he had some forebodings but believed that his seat was safe.

As he had in the past, Frank campaigned hard and covered his riding well. Privately, he told Tamaki it was not as easy as in previous years, but in spite of the complaints he heard from his constituents, he believed he would win. He worked hard on his campaign in Atlin right up until the deadline before election day. Tamaki stayed in Vancouver so she could watch the results from the Vancouver Hotel. From there she could monitor the vote as the ballots were tallied. Because communications in Atlin were poor, Frank would not be able to get the latest figures as the evening wore on. But he would be able to contact her for the latest information. In addition, she would be close by when Frank's plane landed in Vancouver.

The polls closed at nine, and an hour later Frank phoned the Vancouver Hotel. Tamaki was pleased to tell him that it was close but that he was ahead. After she hung up, however, the count began to change, and when he arrived at the hotel a few hours later, believing he had won, she had to tell him that he had lost. She always said it was the hardest thing she ever had to do. An official recount was taken and when the final tally was made it was a heartbreaker for Frank. He had lost his seat in Atlin by one vote to Alan Passarell of the NDP. The recount showed 750 votes for Passarell and 749 for Calder. The most difficult finding of all for him was that many of his own people, the Nisga'a, had not supported him. The only positive result of the entire evening was that it made Tamaki decide to become a Canadian citizen so she could vote. Never before had she realized how important one vote could be. Over and over she kept thinking, "If only I had made the decision sooner when I was in Atlin with Frank I could have voted in the advance poll."

When the number of seats in the legislature was counted it was found that the Social Credit Party had won by five seats. They had taken thirty-one seats with 48 percent of the vote. The NDP had won twenty-six seats and taken 46 percent of the vote.

CHAPTER 15

In Retirement, 1980–2000

FRANK'S LIFE CHANGED dramatically after his defeat in 1979. Knowing that he would be sixty-five years old on August 3 of the following year, he made the decision not to run for political office again. Although he no longer had regular commitments, he was still asked to serve on committees. He also continued to follow the legislative agenda with interest and to work behind the scenes for equal rights for all. To the end of his life, he took an active interest in the affairs of government and remained an unofficial advisor to the Nisga'a Convention. Whenever he could, he was always ready to help in any way possible.

Although Frank no longer sat in the legislature, he was a frequent visitor to the Public Gallery and followed the political scene closely. He was aware that the provincial economy was in poor shape and was causing serious labour strife throughout the province. As Bennett had feared when he had called the election, the economy had become progressively worse, in large part due to the drop in government spending. Frank watched as Social Credit's austerity program, which had been a major cause of his defeat and of that of many Socred candidates, was continued and reinforced. Government revenues were continuing to fall and, since Bennett believed in a balanced budget, that meant cuts to various social programs.

Schools became an especially hot topic. Frank had fought hard for First Nations children to attend public schools and any cut-backs would affect them along with other children. Bennett also decided to change the amount of money allotted to private schools. Money for schools was awarded by an amount per pupil set by the government and paid on September 30 to school boards on the basis of the number of pupils enrolled in a board's district. Previously, religious and other independent schools had received only a small fraction of this amount. In a controversial move, Bennett raised the amount for students in private schools to 60 percent of what public school pupils received, a move that Frank realized would be controversial. Although the government claimed it was fairer and lowered taxes because it saved 40 percent on every child enrolled outside the public system, it made the BC Teachers' Federation furious. Public education had received no increases, and the new measure might encourage more parents to enroll their children in private schools. They charged that the government was undermining universal public education.

Frank had always liked and admired Premier Bill Bennett, but along with most British Columbians he noted that the premier appeared oblivious to the massive discontent he was causing. In the months that followed, the economic situation deteriorated further and labour became increasingly frustrated.[1] In the face of massive opposition, the Socreds held night sessions to get unpopular cut-backs passed as quickly as possible. It ended in the most intense labour conflict the province had ever known.

A "Solidarity Coalition" led by the BC Federation of Labour and supported by the BC Teachers' Federation was formed. People took to the streets in protest marches and attended rallies, but it did nothing to deter the government from its course. By November, Solidarity was planning a general strike. Finally, Jack Munro, then vice-president of the BC Federation of Labour and a highly respected labour leader declared that a general strike was "no walk in the park." He arranged to meet with Premier Bill Bennett in Kelowna and reached an agreement known as the Kelowna Accord. An uneasy peace ensued. Many in the labour movement never forgave the Social Credit Party.

Frank does not appear to have commented publicly on the Solidarity movement, and it is difficult to determine what his stand might have been. On one hand he had never condoned civil disobedience, but on the other hand he had always believed strongly in negotiation. In the past he had negotiated many difficult fishing agreements and believed that middle ground could usually be found. His private opinion was that the situation had been handled poorly. The entire period of mayhem was an all-time low for BC, and along with most people in the province, Calder gave a sigh of relief when a general strike and possible violence were avoided.

At home Frank faced another change. He had completed arrangements for Tamaki's mother to obtain landed immigrant status, and she had arrived to live permanently in Victoria. Frank's house on the Gorge was too small for the three of them, so Tamaki had borrowed money from her mother, and they had bought a larger house on Parkland Drive in Esquimalt. It was not a big house, but it did give Tamaki's mother a room of her own. They rented out the house on the Gorge and used the money to pay back their loan. As had been the case with Frank's first house, one room became his office and he devoted one wall of it to all the honours, awards and commendations he had received during his political life. It was a varied and extensive collection.

An unfortunate consequence of Mrs. Koshibe's arrival was that once she had settled in Canada she spent more time with her daughter and began to emphatically tell Tamaki her genuine opinion of Frank. It became apparent that in reality his mother-in-law had never accepted him and was appalled by her daughter's marriage. In spite of all the help Frank had given her, she began making unfavourable comments about his age, his appearance and his heritage.

Tamaki's mother was not the only person from Japan to come to Victoria at that time. Surprisingly soon, only a year after the Calders had visited his country, Mr. Ohira had become prime minister of Japan. Two years later, in his official capacity he came to Canada. His first stop was Ottawa and after that Vancouver, where, on May 6, 1980, Prime Minister Trudeau held a state dinner in his honour. Frank and Tamaki were invited along with the consul from Japan and many other dignitaries. Frank greatly respected Mr. Trudeau and would be forever grateful for his help following the decision on the Calder Case. He was delighted to be able to see him again seated at the head table on the stage, surprisingly with his young son Justin beside him. When dinner was over and the crowd mingled, Frank was able to talk to the prime minister and renew his acquaintance. Frank had corresponded with Trudeau a number of times over various issues, and Trudeau had always replied warmly, thanking Frank for his encouraging words (see appendix 5).

A year after they moved to Parkland, and much to their delight, Tamaki became pregnant. They decided to sell the Esquimalt house to Tamaki's mother and buy another house on St. David Avenue in Oak Bay. It was roomy and they believed it would be a good place to bring up a child. On December 4, 1982, Tamaki gave birth to a baby boy. He weighed seven pounds, seven ounces, had black hair and, like all babies, had blue eyes but they soon deepened to a dark, rich brown. They named him Erick Arthur Mamoru. They chose "Erick" because it means leader, "Arthur" because it was Frank's middle name and "Mamoru" because it

Frank holding Erick shortly after his son's birth, December 1982.

means "to protect." At Erick's birth, Frank registered him as a member of the Nisga'a First Nation, and because Tamaki had been initiated into the Wolf clan, and children always have the same crest as their mother, Erick automatically took the crest of the Wolf. From the first, Frank spent much time admiring his new son. With wonderment in his voice, Frank told Tamaki: "I believe Erick was sent to us for a very special reason."

As is the case with many parents, the birth of a child changed the focus of Frank's life. He could never say "no" to his son. When Erick was little and Frank was writing a report, if Erick wanted to sit on his lap and type, Frank would stop his work and let him do so until the toddler became bored. He took him often to the shore, and there was a section of Oak Bay Beach that they named "Erick's Beach." On the way home they often stopped at the Windsor Tea Room for lemonade. In winter, if it snowed, Frank took him to the Victoria Golf Club and went sledding with him. As Erick grew older, it was Frank who taught him to ride a bike at a young age when Tamaki thought it was too dangerous. It was Frank who taught him how to play baseball and the finer points of soccer.

When the time for Erick to go to school drew near Tamaki spoke to Frank and said, "Frank sometimes you must say 'no' to Erick. At school he has to understand that he can't always have everything his own way. He will have to share with many other children." Frank shook his head. "I may have only a few years' time to spend with Erick. I don't want to spend them saying 'no.'" Tamaki was the one who had to teach Erick that he could not always have his own way. Frank wanted to enjoy every minute with him while he could.

In his early years, Erick attended St. Christopher's Montessori pre-school program. Before his first day, Tamaki said to him, "You must listen carefully to the way your teachers say words and say them the way they do, not the way I do. I grew up speaking Japanese, not English." St. Christopher's proved to be an excellent preparation for their son. As the time came closer for Erick to enter kindergarten they both knew they had to make a decision. Tamaki attended an information night for parents that presented the basics of different methods of education. She learned about the advantages of the public school system, the Montessori system, the French Immersion program, and the many different philosophies of various private schools. They talked about them together, and after much discussion they decided on St. Michaels University School. The main reasons were that Tamaki's parents had favoured private schools, and Frank knew his parents had considered Coqualeetza an important factor in his upbringing and that of his siblings. Their second reason was that Canada seemed a vast, empty country to Tamaki, and she wanted a close-knit school for him where he would feel safe and secure. They considered that smaller classes would develop a feeling of belonging in him. The third reason was that St. Michaels offered Japanese as a subject, and Erick was half Japanese. They wanted Erick to learn the language and understand that side of his inherited culture.

To further Erick's knowledge of Japanese, when school closed for Christmas and summer holidays, Tamaki flew with him to Japan where she had him attend courses. She did this for a few years beginning when their son was in kindergarten. There, Erick enjoyed classes such as swimming in the summer and skiing in the winter with Japanese children. Both parents believed it was important for Erick to experience his mother's side of his heritage.

When Erick was five, like so many boys he joined Beavers, the junior arm of Boy Scouts. When it was time for the pack to go to camp, they needed fathers to volunteer as leaders. Frank never hesitated and immediately volunteered, even though at the time he was over seventy years of age. He had good skills for the job. He had been a leader in his school days at Coqualeetza, enjoyed the outdoors, and was good with all the boys. Frank slept in a tent, ate food cooked over a campfire and never complained. He described it as a very positive experience.

During an Easter break, Frank took Erick to the Nisga'a lands and taught him how to fish and how to clean and prepare what he caught. It was a time together when he could instruct his son in the lore of his people. Together, they smoked and dried oolichan. He taught Erick why the process had been so important to the Nisga'a. The oil had been used in baking and as butter, and as a cure for small wounds. As well, it had provided light during the dark evenings of the northern winter because it burned well in their oil lamps. While they were there Erick was impressed by the mountain Frank always referred to as Mount Ararat,

Erick when he visited the Nisga'a lands with Frank.
Mount Owe Ka Tahpqwit is in the background.

about which the Nisga'a have an important myth that is somewhat similar to the Biblical story of Noah and the Ark. Years before, Eli Gosnell had told Tamaki the tale, and now Frank told it to Erick.

Frank began by explaining that First Nations people in the northwest tell many stories in which floods are often a central element. He told him that the Nisga'a myth had been recorded in many places and had many variations. In the Haida narrative, it is somewhat different from the one Eli Gosnell had told Tamaki. The recorded version claims the flood was delivered by the Chief of the Sky to punish the Nisga'a for disregarding him and allowing their children to play so noisily they disturbed his sleep.[2] The version told to Erick goes as follows:

"Once many, many years ago there was a great flood in the Nass Valley and the Nisga'a people were in grave danger. The heavy winter snow was melting from the mountains. Great streams were gushing down to the valley below. Day after day the rain fell in torrents and day after day the waters of the rivers crept higher. Slowly, they rose beyond the riverbanks and across the valley floor. Each day they flowed further from the river bed and grew deeper and deeper, and still the mountains streamed water and the rains fell.

"The chief became tormented with worry, for he knew great danger might lie ahead. He called all the Nisga'a together and announced, 'This is no ordinary flood. Never has there been so much water flowing down from the mountains and the skies never clear. It could last for many days and many nights. No one can tell how high the water will come or how far it will spread. We must leave to save our children and ourselves. Pack all the smoked and dried food you possess along with warm clothing and blankets. Take your animals. Fill the largest canoes and paddle to Owe Ka Tahpqwit.[3] It is the highest mountain in the Nass and the snow at its peak never melts so we will all be safe there no matter how high the water rises.'

"The Nisga'a loaded their canoes and paddled to the mountain as their chief had commanded. They tied their canoes to strong rocks so they could not be swept away. There they camped until the waters receded and it was safe to go home again. Because the chief had been wise and because the Nisga'a had obeyed him, their nation was saved. It is said that even to this day the footprints of the Nisga'a who lived on the mountain during the great flood can be seen."[4]

Frank was pleased that Erick had shown interest in the traditional stories of the Nisga'a and hoped that one day he would pass them on to his children. He and Erick enjoyed their time together in the outdoors. Throughout Frank's life he and Erick always remained close and understood each other well.

During his retirement Frank was kept busy. The federal government was considering constitutional changes that would affect First Nations people. He was appointed to a seven-member panel that travelled across Canada to probe the opinions of Aboriginals on the proposed changes. Frank was a valuable member of the team because of his long experience in writing reports and his awareness of how to deal with both First Nations people and those in government. For the same reasons the province of British Columbia appointed him to the Seniors' Advisory Council, formed to study the needs of senior citizens. Both committees required travel and necessitated his being away from home. At other times he was away from home as a guest speaker or at presentation ceremonies. In retirement, year after year he continued to receive recognition for his accomplishments during his long years of political public service. On April 25, 1985, in recognition of his outstanding service to the Nisga'a Nation, the Nisga'a Tribal Council bestowed the title of President Emeritus upon him for life. It gave him full membership on the executive board for his lifetime (see appendix 6).

Another request during these years came from the University of Victoria Faculty of Law. Professor Hamar Foster asked Frank to be a guest lecturer and speak to his first-year law students about Aboriginal issues and especially about the Calder Case. The students, of course, had many questions, and Professor Foster recalls that one of Frank's endearing habits was to begin his answers with the exclamation, "Jeepers." They would go something like this, "Jeepers, when you consider . . ." or "Jeepers I never thought of that. . . ." He was always well received by the students, who particularly enjoyed his stories about his early life and behind-the-scenes events concerning the Calder Case.

The age difference between Frank and Tamaki was more than twenty-five years, and as the years went by it became obvious that there was a price to be paid for it. Most of her friends were her age, and Frank's friends were closer to his age. In addition, their backgrounds were completely different. Since Frank spent much of his time writing reports and articles, or was away travelling for the government, it left Tamaki alone much of the time, and she began to feel that life was becoming monotonous, that she was missing something. She was young and wanted entertainment. Her mother was always nearby and exerted much influence over her. With increasing acidity, Mrs. Koshibe commented on what she saw as Frank's shortcomings. Once she asked Tamaki, "Why are you still with him when he is so much older than you?" Her mother wanted her to leave.

Finally, Tamaki made the decision that they would live apart. Frank did not want the separation because, from his viewpoint, their relationship had always been good, and his religious beliefs were against divorce. He did not see the need nor did he believe it was right. In the end they reached a compromise. They moved to separate homes, but did not craft a formal, legal separation agreement. They made a point of seeing each other twice a week or more, shared Erick, and enjoyed special days as a family. He continued to travel and Tamaki continued to live in the house on St. David Avenue with Erick. After the first few months, Frank moved to a house on Carnarvon Street that was close to St. Michaels School. He chose this location because he wanted to be close to his son.

The separation was hard on Frank. He had high expectations of himself, and their separation, coming as it did after being forced to leave politics, did not come easily for him. As a result, he sometimes drank to excess. Early in their marriage Tamaki saw him drunk once and told him, "Never be drunk in front of me again." She states, "After that he never was." Intellectually he did not agree with immoderate alcohol consumption, but turned to it occasionally when life overwhelmed him. Tamaki remembers the episodes as rare and always away from home.

When Erick was twelve, Tamaki decided that he should do his own laundry, believing it would help him learn to be independent. When Erick went to spend the weekends with Frank he loaded up his laundry bag, slung it over his shoulder, and Tamaki drove him to Frank's. There, his father helped him wash his clothes and showed him how to fold and smooth every garment. When he arrived home there would be a neat, clean pile to be placed in drawers. Erick learned it all from Frank. They even ironed together.

Erick was now in middle school and doing well academically. Unlike Frank he was not a particularly good athlete but like Tamaki he enjoyed music. He developed a good singing voice and could act. He was in many of the school's annual musical presentations at Victoria's McPherson Theatre. His first part was in *Oliver* where he played the part of the Newsboy. At that time his voice was a young boy's soprano but as he matured it became a deep bass. In high school he was the Wizard in *The Wizard of Oz* and the King in *The King and I*. Both parents were very proud of him and always attended his performances. Frank always bought a ticket for each evening his son was on stage so he could attend every night and applaud loudly. Erick continued at St. Michaels until graduation in June of 2000 and from there he went to Queen's University in Ontario where he graduated with honours in Classics. Later, he attended the University of Toronto and received an advanced degree in Archaeology.

In 1988 Frank was made an Officer of the Order of Canada. Elizabeth II, as Queen of Canada, confers the award and the Governor General,

Tamaki, Erick and Frank at UBC when Frank received his
honorary Doctor of Divinity, 1989.

acting as her representative, presents it at an awards ceremony in Government House in Ottawa. The award's Latin motto is *Desiderantes meliorem
patriam*, which means "Desiring a Better Country." It was a fitting motto
to bestow on Frank because he had helped to make Canada a better place
for First Nations by winning land rights for them. Tamaki travelled to
Ottawa with Frank for the presentation, was proud of him, and considered him a very deserving recipient. In 1989 he was invited to the Anglican Theological College at the University of British Columbia where he
received the honorary degree of "D.D.," Doctor of Divinity, Anglican
Church.

Every year in October, he attended the Nisga'a Convention. He continued to speak on important issues and to function as a wise elder to the
Nisga'a. His vast experience was a valuable asset. When he had little else
to do, he kept busy compiling clippings and documents in his scrapbooks.
Tamaki accompanied him to all his awards ceremonies and continued to
be supportive of him. As he grew older they stayed good friends and his
mind remained clear and active. People often said, "When he speaks,
Frank really doesn't seem old," and to those close to him, he never was.

CHAPTER 16

The Nisga'a Treaty, 1991–2000

FRANK HAD BEEN RETIRED for eleven years when discussions for compensation to First Nations for land were initiated. He had spent his life fighting for land title and had waited almost twenty years after the Supreme Court of Canada had heard the Calder Case to see recompense for past wrongs begin. It would be a woman who would initiate the process — a brave move because for years it had been considered that to do so would invite political censure. Premier Rita Johnson, the first woman to become premier of any Canadian province, approved the process but did not stay in office long enough to begin the First Nation land consultation process. She had been elected by the Social Credit Party to replace Premier Bill Vander Zalm after he was forced to resign over a property scandal.[1]

A few months into office, Johnson called an election for October 17, 1991. Some people looked forward to British Columbia having the first elected woman premier in Canada. However, in spite of her catchy campaign chant, "Yay, hey Rita J; Rita J. is here to stay," it was not to be. Not only did she lose her seat, her party was badly defeated. Thereafter, the Social Credit Party slowly disintegrated and never formed another government. Much of the blame was placed on her predecessor Bill Vander Zalm.

Frank saw his old party, the NDP, win a landslide victory of fifty-one seats to Social Credit's seven. It was led by Mike Harcourt, a lawyer and former mayor of Vancouver, and he actually set the land title negotiations in motion. The Nisga'a Nation was first. It was only fair because they had won and paid for the court battles. Nevertheless, the firmly entrenched position of the government on land ownership had not changed. Government still held to the position that private land, parks, right of ways, forest and animal reserves were not negotiable.

The Nisga'a Treaty negotiating team was formed with representatives from all three levels of government. Representatives for the major stakeholders were as follows: the federal government led by Ronald Irwin, minister of Indian Affairs and Northern Development, the provincial government of British Columbia led by John Cashore, minister of Aboriginal Affairs, and the Nisga'a First Nation led by Chief Joseph Gosnell, President of the Nisga'a Convention. Late in 1991 the participants signed an initial agreement setting out the scope of negotiations covering land, resources and compensation.

While Nisga'a negotiations were progressing slowly, three years into Harcourt's term a horrific scandal broke out that eventually forced him to resign. It centred on the Nanaimo Commonwealth Holding Society. This was a supposedly charitable organization, but some of its funds were being siphoned into the pockets of the NDP party. Cash was being withheld from Bingo operations, expenses were often paid in cash, and when donations to charities were made, kickbacks were required. A nun, Sister Mary Rowe, furious at the scam, complained to the media. She stated, "eight hundred dollars has to be kicked back for every thousand [she] received, or [her] funding dried up."[2]

Ronald Parks, appointed to investigate the situation, was a forensic accountant with the firm of Lindquist, Avey, Macdonald, Baskerville. He found accounts so tangled that it was difficult to discover where all the money had actually gone. In court, David Stupich, a past NDP president, an elected member of parliament and a member of the legislature in

Victoria was found guilty of stealing almost a million dollars. He was the only person convicted though many must have been involved. Parks estimated that from 1974 to 1988 only 5 percent of revenues had gone to charity.[3] Premier Harcourt claimed he knew nothing about the scheme but resigned in November of 1995. Nevertheless, the Nisga'a owed Harcourt a debt of gratitude because he started the bargaining process for land title that had been approved by the former government. The NDP party elected Glen Clark to finish out Harcourt's term.

Land negotiations proceeded but were barely noticed by the general public. Media attention was focused on ongoing political scandals. Little by little, however, discussions struggled forward. Over two hundred and fifty consultations and public information meetings were held between 1992 and 1998. The participants met hundreds of times in many different places, including New Aiyanish, Greenville, Victoria, Vancouver, Terrace and Prince Rupert. The purpose of the geographical diversification was to give the public as much opportunity as possible to observe and become informed. In most places few people paid attention.

Frank Calder was an exception. He was not at the negotiating table but he kept himself well informed every step of the way. After all, it had been his life's mission to "move that mountain," the apparently unmovable mountain that represented land title to the Nisga'a people. Frank was gratified to see compensation finally coming to fruition.

After years of intense negotiations, on August 4, 1998, the delegates of the three levels of government announced they had reached agreement in principle. Representatives of the Nisga'a First Nation, the government of British Columbia and the government of Canada initialled an agreed-upon document.[4] The major terms stated that the Nisga'a Nation collectively would be given almost two thousand square kilometres of land in the Nass Valley. This was only 8 percent of what they had originally claimed were their ancestral holdings. In addition, $190 million would be paid to them in compensation, of which $11.5 million were reserved for upgrading their commercial fisheries. They were guaranteed a share of fish, timber, animal and mineral resources. They would receive rights to a form of self-government that a central Nisga'a government would administer and include all four villages.

Historically there had been no centralization and each village had managed its own affairs and had had its own chief. The treaty would make a significant change. A central Nisga'a government would manage health care, social services and education for the entire nation. To do this they would receive $32 million a year from the federal government in transfer payments and contribute to this amount from their own funds. Over time, the amount of the transfer payment would be reduced and the Nisga'a contribution increased. In return, the Nisga'a agreed to give up their exemption from taxation under the Indian Act and agreed that no further land claims based on Aboriginal land title would be filed.[5]

Frank had enough reservations about the final terms that when the vote came to the Nisga'a people he voted against the document, even though its recognition that there must be compensation for past grievances was a great satisfaction to him. The Calder Case had made the claim possible, but the Nisga'a Treaty would grant legal acknowledgement that the wrong committed deserved recompense.

Four steps of ratification remained before the treaty would become law. It required approval by the Nisga'a First Nation people, the provincial Legislature, the federal House of Commons and the Senate.

First a referendum was held for the Nisga'a. Voting stations were established on November 6 and 7, 1998, in four villages: New Aiyanish, Canyon City, Greenville and Kincolith. New Aiyanish, where Joe Gosnell lived, the chief who had led the team as the chief Nisga'a negotiator, passed it with over 80 percent in favour. The count in the other three villages was much closer, and some Nisga'a were actually hostile to the terms and refused to vote. The final count was 1,451 (61 percent) in favour, 558 (23 percent) opposed and 356 (15 percent) abstentions.[6]

While the vote was being conducted, the popularity of the government and the status of Premier Clark were plummeting. Desperate to bolster his image before again facing the electorate, he needed a triumph and believed that the Nisga'a Treaty might be one means by which it might happen. The premier needed speedy ratification by the legislature if this was to happen before he had to call an election.

The first step of the process, passage by the Nisga'a had been successful. The second and the one that concerned Clark most was passage by the Legislative Assembly of British Columbia. The first reading was tabled on November 30, 1998. First readings are mainly a formality to acquaint the house with the content and issues of a bill. From there the matter quickly proceeds to committee, followed by second reading, and debate by all members of the legislature. The second reading was introduced the very next day on December 1. Immediately, controversy erupted as Calder watched from the Public Gallery.

During the formative years of the treaty there had been little information in the media for the public to examine. Attention had been focused elsewhere, mainly on scandals. The final agreement came as a surprise even to members of the legislature, and seemed extreme to many. Opponents decried it on the following issues:

– Provisions for self-government created a new level of government;
– Self-government for a group within Canada changed the Canadian constitution and therefore required a province-wide referendum;
– The treaty created a fishery based on race (a charge made by commercial fishers);
– The Gitskan stated that part of their territory had been given to the Nisga'a and filed a claim accordingly.

They were serious charges and a legislative committee was appointed to study the document and prepare it for debate in the house. It was obvious there would be much controversy.[7]

Even though Calder was gratified the treaty had recognized that compensation was necessary, he was one of those opposed to some of the terms. He did not have a seat in the house, nor did he have a direct voice with the negotiators, but he had great influence with his people. He used it where he could. Frank had always favoured municipal style government, which the negotiated terms had not specified. As well, he believed the treaty gave too much power to a central Nisga'a government. For example, the government would have the power to decide who was a Nisga'a citizen and who could vote and who could not. Even though Tamaki was Frank's wife, and had been initiated into the Nisga'a Nation as a princess, she was denied voting privileges. The basis of denial was that she did not have Nisga'a blood.

In addition, Frank questioned whether the Nisga'a had been granted enough land on which to earn a decent living. The traditional grounds his family had hunted when he was growing up had not been included. He wanted his people to be self-sufficient. He believed that before the document was legislated more time was needed to rally divergent opinions and discuss the finer points. Shortly, the house closed for over three weeks to celebrate Christmas and the New Year.

The legislature reopened in the second week of January 1999. During the holiday recess, the committee appointed to study the Nisga'a Treaty and guide it through the legislature had prepared twenty-two chapters for debate. Following the usual practice, one by one they would present them to the house.

The opening, however, coincided with another scandal that had first reared its head before the Christmas break and now erupted violently in the media. It concerned an application for a gaming license for a casino in Burnaby, BC. A friend and neighbour of Premier Glen Clark named Dimitrios Pilarinos along with a few other investors had made the application. It looked suspiciously like cronyism. A former Appeals Court judge, Martin Taylor, was appointed as special prosecutor to look into the case, and the RCMP began staking out residences, tapping phone lines and using other methods of surveillance to investigate the matter. It made enticing reading in newspapers and completely obscured the Nisga'a Treaty.

By March the license for the casino scandal had broken out in force. The RCMP raided Clark's home at 7 P.M. on the second day of the month. BCTV crews and a reporter named John Daly were outside his home and recorded the event. Daly insisted he and his crew were there on a hunch, and the RCMP supported them by claiming they had no inkling the crews would be there.[8] Denials and acrimonious accusations flew across the floor of the legislature. On March 16, the premier's office in Victoria was searched. The Nisga'a Treaty was supplanted by far more sensational news.

Nevertheless, the business of the legislature progressed slowly, with chapter after chapter of the Nisga'a Treaty being discussed in detail. By April 21 only eleven of the twenty-two issues had been debated. As opposition mounted, led by Liberal Gordon Campbell, a future premier,

Clark declared the process was becoming far too slow, and he invoked closure. On April 21, he made a motion to that effect in the house and gave a lengthy speech in support of it. He concluded with these words, "I'm proud to close debate. I'm proud to move third reading."[9] It was Clark's legal right to do so, but it was an extreme measure. Closure is a tactic that is seldom used except in emergency situations. Calder, along with many others, was appalled. It ended all argument on the treaty and chapters twelve to twenty-two never came under the scrutiny of provincial representatives. The next day Minister of Finance Joy MacPhail called for the third and final reading. It passed by a vote of 37 in favour to 29 opposed.[10]

Frank had been shocked by the use of closure because there was not a deadline for acceptance of the treaty. The land question had been in existence for over a hundred years. Along with many, he was asking, What difference could a few more months make? There will be many more treaties to follow and wouldn't it be best to make the first a sound template for subsequent treaties? A writer for the *Vancouver Province* newspaper, Michael Smyth, on April 23, 1999, sided strongly with this view in an article titled "Calder a Man of Principle: Nisga'a Leader could Give Clark Lessons." In the article he quotes Calder as saying, "They forced the reserves on us. They forced the Indian Act on us. Now with the first modern-day treaty west of the Rocky Mountains — closure. It's coercion.... At the beginning, I supported the premier when he said there would be a thorough discussion. He changed his view, but I retained mine." Smyth continued in his own words, "Brave words from a brave man. I hope they echo in the minds of the New Democrats who forced this treaty through the house yesterday.... It was all orchestrated to give Clark a badly needed photo opportunity at next week's Nisga'a Convention."[11]

A well-known Victoria reporter and columnist, Jim Hume, also agreed with Frank, writing in *The Islander*: "Trust him [Clark] but while trusting him, listen to Nisga'a elder Frank Calder who sat as an MLA from 1949 to 1979 and understood the meaning of closure far better than Clark or Wilson or Nisga'a Chief Joe Gosnell. Hereditary Chief Calder said he would rather have waited a while longer for legislative ratification of the treaty. He worried about the impression closure would create throughout British Columbia and in Ottawa when the treaty reaches the House of Commons for debate. He is wise to be worried."

Clark at the Nisga'a Convention the next month announced the passage of the treaty by both the Nisga'a Nation and the legislature of British Columbia. He praised it as a great, historic first. He was rewarded with pictures in newspapers throughout the province and across Canada of himself standing at the podium. Ratification was still needed by both the House of Commons and the Senate in Ottawa.

On August 22, Premier Clark resigned because he could no longer function in office. His credibility had been too badly shaken on too many issues. In addition to the casino scandal, the three fast-cat ferries (catamarans) he had approved for purchase when he was minister of transport under Harcourt were an economic disaster. If they had proved a success, they might have been a great step forward in BC transportation, but unfortunately, after purchasing them for millions, they never functioned properly. Additional millions were spent on repairs and storage. The two premiers elected by the NDP to serve out Clark's term, Dan Miller and Ujjal Dosanjh, were affected by the fast-cat scandal as well, and they were in office only a short time. The session finally ended and, as had previously happened with Vander Zalm, Clark was charged in court. Neither premier received anything more than a reprimand, and both were acquitted of all criminal charges.

It remained for the federal government to pass the Nisga'a Treaty. This was not an easy process. In all, 471 amendments were proposed in the House of Commons. In spite of lengthy objections to some points of restitution by Reform Party members, causing late-night sittings spent in heated debate, on December 13, the Nisga'a Treaty was passed by the House of Commons without a single amendment being approved.

The only hurdle remaining was the Senate. The timing for the bill in the Senate was poor because the winter break started almost immediately afterwards and would last until February. It was not until April 2000, that the Senate debated the bill and voted in favour. It was left only for the Governor General, Adrienne Clarkson, on April 13 to sign the Nisga'a Final Agreement Act into law. It took affect on May 11, 2000. It was twenty-seven years after the House of Commons had voted to recognize First Nation land title, thus breaking the tie the Supreme Court of Canada had handed down in the Calder Case.

In the nine years from the beginning of Nisga'a Treaty negotiations in 1991 to the final passage in 2000 provincial politics had been extremely chaotic. The province had had six different premiers, four of whom had been forced to resign. It began with the scandal involving Premier Bill Vander Zalm and proceeded to a rash of discovery of wrong-doing by succeeding governments.

Some questions that can never be answered are as follows: if government and media attention had not been focused elsewhere would Calder have been able to have more influence over the content of the Nisga'a Treaty? If closure had not been invoked could the principles of treaty settlement have been delineated so as to serve as a template for treaties to follow? Throughout the process not one voice was raised saying principles of settlement or equality of compensation should be established to guide negotiations with other First Nations. As a result, every subsequent negotiation has begun anew, which has resulted in prolonged, laborious, expensive contract procedures.

The Nisga'a people were gratified when the Final Agreement Act became law. They had waited a long time for compensation. It was an historic landmark, and to mark its passage the Nisga'a and the BC government developed a special public ceremony of thanks. Victoria High School's vice-principal, Mr. Barry Rolston, arranged one of the performances for an assembly of the school's students. In late May at the back of the school's auditorium, through double doors carved in a First Nation design almost eight years earlier, Dr. Frank Calder and ten other Nisga'a slowly entered the dimmed auditorium. All were dressed in full Nisga'a regalia. On stage to rhythmic drumming they began the ceremony by thanking the great spirits for their land and promising always to respect it. Much of the chanting was in Nisga'a, and even though the student body did not understand the words, they felt the strong emotion. Throughout the presentation the body of teenagers sat hushed. Students who attended recalled it as a very moving experience. For Frank it was a celebration of his life's work.

The Nisga'a Treaty was a Canadian landmark and made a considerable impact across the country. Today around the world in many countries Aboriginal negotiations are taking place, and Canada is looked upon as a leader in the field. People from all walks of life visit the Nisga'a lands to tour and take workshops on the process. Workshops cover many topics including but not limited to the following: the contents of the treaty; interrelationships of negotiating parties' interests; the ratification rounds; strategic communications and public education.

The opening statement in the information provided by the Nisga'a Lisims Government website is as follows: "The objective of treaty negotiation should be to enable a First Nation to preserve its culture, while maintaining enough territory, resources and authority to provide its people with a reasonable prospect of prosperity achieved through its own efforts and resources.[12] It is a statement with which Frank fully agreed.

CHAPTER 17

He Will Move that
Mountain

IN MAY 2000 AFTER THE Senate passed the Nisga'a Treaty and it became law, Frank's life work was complete. He had triumphed after 113
years of resistance to colonial, provincial and federal governments by his
people. The Calder Case had been the pinnacle of his career, and the treaty
was the reward he had made possible for all First Nations. He would
have negotiated some terms differently, but inwardly he felt a deep satisfaction with the results of his efforts. He had fulfilled the almost impossible prediction of his father Chief Na-qua-oon when he said, "He will
move that mountain."

Once the Nisga'a Treaty became law, Tamaki began to think back on
all the long years of her husband's effort. Pondering those years, she wrote
the following words that beautifully describe the progression of Frank's
life:

> His father said to the crowd of men and women,
> "One day, this boy can walk like a white man,
> eat like a white man,

speak like a white man.
Then, he shall move that mountain."

One day, he was sent to the place of the unknown.
He worked there,
He strived there
To comply with his father's wish to become a man
Who walks like a white man
eats like a white man
speaks like a white man.

Years later he became a man
Who worked hard
For the people who were in need,
For the place where his services were required.

Sometimes he was deceived,
Sometimes he was ignored.
He survived.
He was a very forgiving man.

His hard work continued,
walking like a white man,
eating like a white man,
speaking like a white man.

Many years later
The day finally came.
Though the result was not the way he intended.
That day, his life work indeed moved a mountain.
He had fulfilled his father's wish, finally.
He had moved that mountain.[1]

In his later years prestigious awards continued to be bestowed upon Frank. In 2004, four years after the treaty was signed, he received the Order of British Columbia at Government House in Victoria. The award had been established in April 1989 to recognize "those people who have served with great distinction and excelled in any field of endeavour benefiting the people of British Columbia." It is the highest award bestowed by the province. It was followed later the same year by his second doctor-

Frank with three of his sisters, Winifred, Dorothy and Thelma,
after receiving the Order of British Columbia, 2004.

ate. The University of Victoria bestowed upon him the title of Doctor of
Laws. The year 2004 was a proud one for Dr. Calder.

In August of that year, Frank would be ninety but remained as clear-
minded and as interested in life as ever. His age, however, was slowly
beginning to tell, and as the years slipped by, Tamaki began to realize
that he needed more care than she could provide for him at home and
began to consider what would happen as he aged even more.

Tamaki continued to visit Japan every year, and when she was away
always worried about Frank staying alone. In 2005 this problem became
critical. At the end of August, she had reservations to fly to Japan. The
week before she was to leave, she and Frank were getting ready to have
one of their twice-weekly lunches together. The time arrived for them to
leave the house, and Frank was not even dressed. He was still in his
nightshirt, which was most extraordinary. Usually he was ready and
waiting, wearing a meticulously clean white shirt and freshly pressed
suit. That day he did not even care whether they went or not. All he
wanted was to take his wife into his office to talk and discuss some documents with her.

In his office, he unlocked a steel file box and took out files one by one
and opened each in turn. The first was about pensions, the next was his
will and another was the deed for the Ross Bay Cemetery plot he had

The ceremony at the University of Victoria when Frank received
his honorary Doctor of Laws, 2004.

purchased years ago. When he was finished he sat down hard and put his
hands to his head and said, "I feel so dizzy." Tamaki knew there must be
something seriously wrong; this wasn't like Frank at all. She couldn't
leave him alone. Quickly she had to make some arrangement for him
before leaving. She went to many places but most would not take him
because they did not provide the level of care he needed. Finally, she
found Sunrise Assisted Living on Humboldt Street in Victoria. It looked
nice, had space available immediately, and would give him good care.
Frank seemed happy with the new arrangement.

She went to Japan but when she returned in the middle of September
she knew immediately that Frank had not improved. She took him to
the doctor he had had for many years. Extensive medical tests showed he
had cancer of the abdomen. She immediately checked him into the Royal
Jubilee Hospital for an operation that was performed only a few days
later. It was successful and he returned to Sunrise to recuperate. His
friends and his family thought there was an excellent chance of a full
recovery.

Frank enjoyed life at Sunrise. In the dining room, each resident had
an assigned seat at a table. One man at his table was Mr. Olivier Abrioux
who had been born in Aberdeen, Scotland, and before retirement had

Erick's graduation at Queen's University, with Honours in Classics.

been a professor of French language and literature at the University of Victoria. He had taught at universities around the world and had many interesting stories to tell. His son was presently the director at St. Michaels Middle School, which provided a bond since Erick had attended there. They became good friends and received much pleasure from the time they spent together. Frank was especially pleased when he learned that Erick had graduated with Honours in Classics from Queen's University.

In May of the following year, Frank, along with Mr. Hubert Doolan, was invited to Greenville to unveil a plaque to commemorate the opening of Nisga'a Highway 113 at Gitwinksihlkw in the Nass Valley. It had been named "Number 113" for the one hundred and thirteen years it had taken the Nisga'a to attain title to their land. The dedication ceremony would take place on May 3, 2006. As Frank was very frail, Tamaki did not want him to go, but he was determined. She thought about it a great deal, and finally came to the conclusion that if he died along the way he would die happy because he would be doing what he wanted to do.

Frank took the bus to Terrace because he wanted to see the scenery in that part of the world one more time. There he was met by a car and driver and taken to Greenville. The ceremony meant much to Frank because highways for the North were one of the issues he had fought hard for in the legislature. He returned to Sunrise happy and was no worse off for having taken the trip.

At Sunrise, Frank was determined to live life to its fullest in the time he had left. The next month in June, he attended a dinner for former MLAs at Government House. Shortly afterwards, he was back at the official residence when he was invited to the annual ceremony of the Order of British Columbia. Recipients from the previous year are always invited the following year. He was experiencing some bloating in his abdomen, which made his suit somewhat uncomfortable, but he ignored any discomfort.

In late August he updated his will. Mr. Ian Izard acted for him. He left a very simple document stating his wish to be cremated and to have his ashes buried in Ross Bay Cemetery. Everything he owned he left to his wife and, when he showed the will to her, it brought tears to her eyes. All their married life he had always done the best he could to make her happy. Soon afterwards he gathered together all the gifts, artifacts and awards he had received in his lifetime and had them evaluated. They did not amount to as much as he had expected.

The bloating in Frank's abdomen increased, and when Tamaki went to visit him he would joke, "I'm getting fat." It reached the point where he had to be taken to Victoria General Hospital and have a second operation to drain the fluid. During the process it was found that the cancer had spread. He remained in Victoria General for about three weeks. At the end of that time he could not return to Sunrise because his condition had deteriorated to the point where Sunrise did not have the facilities to care for him. Tamaki was advised to apply for hospice care. Of the choices available, Saanich Peninsula Hospital seemed best to her because it was a smaller place than most and had pleasant surroundings, with a supportive staff. Frank's mind was still clear, and he needed no help signing himself in.

After Frank had been there for two days, he asked Tamaki exactly where the hospital was located. She got a map out and showed him. Immediately, he was worried about how far she had to drive. He had always considered her to be a poor driver. Together they traced a route from Victoria to the hospital that would not require her to drive on the freeway. This pacified Frank somewhat but the last words he said to her at the end of every visit were, "Drive carefully."

Frank received excellent care in the hospice and had a steady stream of visitors, with whom he could converse with intelligence. On one visit, Frank said to Tamaki, "I was born poor and I will die poor." She could tell he was worried, and replied by saying, "The legacy of the accomplishments you leave and how they will improve life for those who come after you are riches far greater than any amount of money could bring." Frank's condition deteriorated to the point where he could not feed himself, and kind volunteers in the hospital took over the job. One day about two weeks later, one of the volunteers stopped Tamaki in the hall and asked, "What is the significance of November 4?"

She thought for a minute and then replied, "I don't know. Frank's birthday is in August and we were married in February. I can't think of anything important that happened on November 4." The volunteer shrugged. "He keeps mentioning that date."

Slowly, Tamaki began to accept that Frank was ready to go, and she believed Frank knew it would not be long. She said to him, "It is all right if you go because then we can be together always." In his last days he became quite philosophical. During one visit he said to Tamaki, "There are many things that happened in my life but there was always a reason. I remember the good things well." Another time he said to her, "Someday, it may be possible to live in both worlds." She'd always thought Frank had lived successfully in both worlds — native and white — but perhaps he had struggled more than he had ever let anyone realize. All

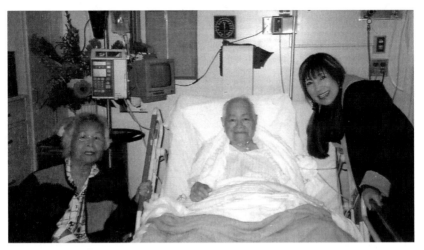

Frank towards the end of his life in hospice care at Saanich Peninsula Hospital.
His sister Dorothy and Tamaki are with him, 2006.

his life he had tried to take an optimistic view of events, even when they must have hurt him deeply, but it had taken a toll.

Frank died quietly on November 4, 2006 — the date he had earlier asked about. Following his wishes, he was cremated, and afterwards his ashes were interred in Ross Bay Cemetery. He had chosen Ross Bay many years before because it was the historical cemetery in Victoria where such people as Sir James Douglas and Emily Carr had been buried. It was a place where people frequently walked, and he hoped some might stop at his grave and ask, "Who was he?" The answer he hoped would lead them to learn that First Nations people had also contributed to the history of British Columbia.

Tamaki arranged for his memorial service to take place on November 16 in Christ Church Cathedral on Quadra Street in Victoria. She did not speak, but in the Order of Service she included the poem she had written about Frank describing his life's progress. The Very Reverend Dr. Logan McMenamie, Rector of Christ Church Cathedral and Dean of Columbia, officiated. Many people attended the service, including many dignitaries. There were those from the world of politics, from his Nisga'a family and from the Anglican clergy.

Frank's son Erick gave the eulogy. He spoke touchingly of his memories of his father. Among other things he said, "Recently, I started to get extremely sentimental about my dad and the times we had spent together. . . . Here is a list of actions and things that stand out to me. Teaching me how to throw a baseball, kick a soccer ball and ride a bike. Walks to our beach and skipping stones into the Strait of Georgia. Watching Bond movies and Star Trek on the downstairs TV. Helping him in the garden and giving up in exhaustion or boredom while he continued to rake leaves, chop wood and dig up weeds . . . his love of silk flowers and his belief that they were superior to real ones, buying bulk candy at Eaton's, waking up to the smell of his BLT's on the weekend. Listening to my dad hum a classic or original tune to himself as he kept time with a slippered foot. Our mutual love of buffets . . . birthdays, anniversaries, school plays, recitals, award ceremonies. I saw him on stage, he saw me on stage."

More than a thousand obituaries appeared in newspapers and magazines across the country and throughout the world. The commendations were high. From a small native village on the remote Nass River, where, before the age of nine he had never seen a car, bus, streetcar or city light, he rose to be one of the leading citizens of his province. The *Victoria Times Colonist* devoted the front of its weekend magazine section to his life.[2] Praise echoed across Canada. The *Aboriginal Newspaper of British Columbia and the Yukon* hailed "Dr. Frank Calder as a 'Hero of Our Time.'" Shawn Atleo, then the regional chief of the BC Assembly of First Nations, said, "It is our duty to be students of men like Calder." Iona Campagnolo, lieutenant governor of British Columbia at the time, commented, "Few of us are privileged to change history; Frank Calder is one who has done so."

Frank never wavered from his conviction of what he believed was right. It was a lonely path, and often he paid a high price for his principles. He stood against many of his own people when he supported the White Paper. He lost in provincial court twice before proceeding to the Supreme Court of Canada to fight for Aboriginal land title. He defied his own party when he fought the unions for inclusion of Aboriginals in their membership and in the pressure he applied to begin land claims negotiations. He never asked for preferential treatment but he wanted a level playing field for all. He believed that if First Nations people achieved this, in time they could live independently of aid. Education, he believed, was the key but he realized it would take time.

On November 4, 2006, in his ninety-second year K'amligihahlhaahl, the Chief of the Heavens, came for him. Somehow Frank had known that November 4 would be the day. Was it because he had been born a dream child carrying the spirit of the dead son of Chief Na-qua-oon? Tamaki sat quietly beside his bed, and the words the fortune teller had foretold so long ago came back to her: "She will make her mark in a distant land." The prophecy had come true. Perhaps she and Frank had always been destined to meet.

Frank's story is remarkable. It is one that began in myth and ended in myth. Hard fought! Hard won! "He moved that mountain."

DR. FRANK A. CALDER,
D.D. LL.D. O.C. O.B.C. A.O.C. L.TH.

DEGREES & HONOURS

L.TH   Licentiate in Theology, University of B. C. Vancouver, 1946
A.O.C. Aboriginal Order of Canada, Carleton University, Ottawa, 1985
D.D.   Doctor of Divinity, Anglican Church, Vancouver, 1989
O.C.   Order of Canada, Ottawa, 1988
O.B.C. Order of British Columbia, Government House, Victoria, 2004
LL.D.   Doctor of Laws, University of Victoria, 2004

FIRST ABORIGINAL IN CANADA

- to graduate from a public high school
- to graduate from the University of British Columbia
- to be elected to any legislature or parliament (26 years)
- to be appointed a cabinet minister

ADDITIONAL HONOURS

- founded the Nisga'a Tribal Council, 1955
- named "Chief of Chiefs" of the Nisga'a, 1958
- admitted to the Canadian First Nations Hall of Fame, Montreal, 1968
- received the National Aboriginal Lifetime Achievement Award, Winnipeg, 1996

OFFICE OF THE MAYOR
July 10, 1962

P.J. Lester, Mayor

City Hall, Fulton Street,
PRINCE RUPERT, B.C.

Mr. Frank Calder, M.L.A.,
1340 East 8th Avenue,
City.

Dear Frank:

I would like to congratulate you on the success of your campaign to secure equality in liquor rights for natives. I think that you handled this program masterfully and have accomplished something which nobody else in the Province had previously been able to do. Your strategy left the Attorney-General with no other choice but to accede to your request.

The granting of equality in liquor rights is the first step towards equality in other fields.

Yours truly

P. J. Lester,
Mayor

APPENDIX 3

P 291-10

Victoria

August 22nd,
1 9 6 2

Frank Calder, Esq., M.L.A.,
Box 243,
Prince Rupert, B.C.

Dear Frank:

Thank you for your letter of July
9th, which has just arrived. In the matter
of suggested policing of Reserves.

I will ask our Police officials to
let me have their reaction these suggestions,
and in the meanwhile, thank you for drawing to
my attention the views of the Nishga Tribal
Council, as presented by their motion of July
7th last.

Yours truly,

R.W. Bonner,
Attorney-General

The following material found in Frank Calder's scrapbook was written by Frank at the age of nine. It is interesting for what it says about the young boy's understanding of Nisga'a marriage customs but even more interesting for what it says about his level of English at the time he left the Nass Valley for school. Naturally, the young boy would soon, through his schooling, become fully proficient in the language.

Heathen Way of Marriage

There are three way of marriage among the heathens, first, common class, when the young man is of age that is over 20 years old his uncle, and the boy's father and all the clan, will chose the right girl for the boy, and next is to give the marriage present to the girl's mother than the girl's mother will have to return all this present back. by means that she really want to know if the boy's family mean what they are doing. and if they boy's family give out the present again, than the father of the said girl will set the date, and the boy will stay with his future in-laws, as I mention before, and when the time comes, the boy will sleep with the girl, till morning, but they are not suppose to get up till some one will ask them to. then of couarse the real marriage present passed to all the girl's clan, after the girl's clan give all kinds of food to the boy, this he use to invite all the heathens for a wedding feast. same way today. high way of marriage, is to run away with the girl, but not her future husband, it's his uncles and brothers that ran away with the girl, that is after everything is set. high class marriage. This is more of a fun, for every one in the Village watch the show, This way of marriage is only used when the Prince and Princess are going to be married. the girl stand with her Uncle at the door while her clans stands ready for battle. her future husband stand back of his clans, their too ready for battle. When the time is set, their all start in, the boy's side try to take the Girl, while her clan keep the others from taken her, all the Villagers stand back and watch the show, women and men on both side get into real fun till the boy side take the Girl . than it's all over, big feast after. no body get hurt. The way of mariage among the Indians, are good, for none of them will need hand out. for the two familys are helping each other all through their lives.

Our Uncle call us at night, and taught us how to live, not to be proud, and always help old man or woman, if they need help. by doing they give us they blessing, to live longer. and to invite any stranger, and give then to eat, and not to talk back to old timers, if they fine we done wrong. also not to laugh at any one who is helpless, but help them and ask for no pay.
—Weinal'th [in Nisga'a means Big Black Fish]

Frank was a member of the killer whale clan, and orcas at that time were commonly referred to as Black Fish. The original was typed in red ink and this copy has used the original spelling and punctuation. Phillip, Frank's brother, thinks he wrote it shortly after going to Coqualeetza, perhaps as an essay assignment.

APPENDIX 5

CANADA

MAR - 9 1977'

PRIME MINISTER · PREMIER MINISTRE

Ottawa, K1A 0A2,
March 2, 1977.

Dear Mr. Calder:

Upon my return from Washington,
your kind letter of February 11 was brought
to my attention. I would like to thank you
sincerely for your personal words of encouragement
and advice regarding my address to a joint session
of the United States Congress. I am enclosing a
copy of the speech which I thought you might like
to have.

Please accept my congratulations to
you and your wife Tamaki on your recent wedding.

Sincerely,

Mr. Frank Calder, M.L.A.,   Pierre Elliott Trudeau
   Legislative Assembly,
      Parliament Buildings,   PRIME MINISTER OF CANADA
         Victoria, B.C.

APPENDIX 6

Nishga Tribal Council

New Aiyansh, B.C., V0J 1A0
Phone 633-2215

NISHGA TRIBAL COUNCIL
28TH ANNUAL CONVENTION
APRIL 25, 1985 - GREENVILLE

RESOLUTION #7

MOVED BY JAMES GOSNELL, SECONDED BY ROD ROBINSON

BE IT RESOLVED:

THAT at this 28th Annual Convention, the Nishga Nation bestow on
Mr. Frank Calder, the first elected President of the Nishga Tribal
Council, the title of PRESIDENT EMERITUS and confer upon him, full
membership to the NTC Executive Board for life, in recognition of
his long services to the Nishga Nation, and for his untiring efforts
towards the recognition of Aboriginal Title and Rights for all Aboriginal Peoples in Canada.

CARRIED UNANIMOUSLY

James Gosnell	Alan Moore	Rev. Ian McKenzie
Rod Robinson	Henry McKay	Larry Guno
Percy Tait	George Nelson	Edmond Wright
Hubert Doolan	Henry Stephens	Nelson Leeson
Joseph Gosnell	Hubert Haldane	
Herbert Morven	Tommy Dennis	
Harry Nyce	Ben Stewart	
Jacob Nyce	Willard Martin	

NOTES

CHAPTER 1: The Early Years (pp. 3–14)

1 Phillip and Dorothy Clark (Frank Calder's siblings), interview by author, July 2008.
2 Yuri Semyonov, *Siberia: Its Conquest and Development*, trans. J.R. Foster (Montreal: International Publishers, 1963), 157.
3 Ibid., 161.
4 Ibid., 211.
5 Barry M. Gough, *Gunboat Frontier: British Maritime Authority and Northwest Coast Indians, 1846–90* (Vancouver: UBC Press, 1984), 190.
6 Margaret Ormsby, *British Columbia: A History* (Vancouver/Toronto: Macmillan, 1958), 69.
7 Unpublished diary of missionaries at Greenville.
8 E. Palmer Patterson, "Kincolith's First Decade: A Nisga'a Village (1867–1878)" online at *brandonu.ca/library/CJNS/12.2/Patterson.pdf* (accessed January 18, 2013).
9 Ibid.
10 Ibid.
11 Alex Rose, *Spirit Dance at Meziadin: Chief Joseph Gosnell and the Nisga'a Treaty* (Madeira Park: Harbour, 2001), 156.
12 "Papers Relating to the Commission appointed to enquire into the state and condition of the Indians of the North-West Coast of British Columbia," February 22, 1883, 432.
13 Hamar Foster, with Heather Raven & Jeremy Webber, *Let Right Be Done: Aboriginal Title, the Calder Case, and the Future of Indigenous Rights* (Vancouver: UBC Press, 2007), 39.
14 Cole Harris, *Making Native Space: Colonialism, Resistance, and Reserves in British Columbia* (Vancouver: UBC Press, 2002), 169.
15 Hamar Foster, 62.

CHAPTER 2: Schooling (pp. 15–24)

1 Public School Act, 1872, in British Columbia, online at viu.ca/homeroom/content/Topics/Statutes/1872act.htm (accessed February 2, 2013).

2 History of Indian Residential Schools, online at clfns.com/images/people/documents/history_of_indian_residential_schools.pdf (accessed February 2, 2013).

3 Coqualeetza Institute (Residential Schools: Sardis, BC), online at co-qualeetza.com (accessed January 30, 2012).

4 "Native People, Political Organization and Activism," in *The Canadian Encyclopedia*, 2nd ed., vol. III (Edmonton: Hurtig, 1988), 1457.

5 Ibid.

6 CBC News (Canada), A History of Residential Schools in Canada, online at cbc.ca/news/canada/story/2008/05/16/f-faqs-residential-schools.html (accessed January 3, 2013).

7 Gerald A. Rushton, *Whistle Up the Inlet: The Union Steamship Story* (Vancouver: J.J. Douglas, 1974), 1–2.

8 Ibid., 91.

9 Ibid., 107.

10 Phillip Calder, interview by author, July 2007.

11 Tamaki Calder, interview by author, September 2010. Tamaki said that Frank sometimes reminisced about school as they chatted in the evenings.

12 Frank Calder, Scrapbook #1 (1936–1952). Many of the details of Frank's schooling are from his first scrapbook along with interviews with his brother Phillip and his wife Tamaki, in her recollection of conversations with him.

13 Ibid.

14 Phillip Calder, interview by author, July 2007.

15 *Totem Yearbook, 1952–53* (University of BC: publication of the Alma Mater Society, 1953), 36.

16 Frank Calder, Scrapbook #1 (1936–1952). Includes UBC newspaper article "Soccer Men Stop Store Squad 4-1" in which Frank and other players are described as a returning team stars.

17 *Call to the Fourteenth Annual Convention: Native Brotherhood and Native Sisterhood of British Columbia* (Cape Mudge, BC: Agenda of Native Brotherhood and Native Sisterhood of BC, 1943).

CHAPTER 3: The First Elections, 1949–1953 (pp. 25–36)

1 Margaret A. Ormsby, *British Columbia: A History* (Vancouver/Toronto: Macmillan, 1958), 475–477.

2 Ibid. 492.

3 "Native People, Political Organization and Activism," in *The Canadian Encyclopedia*, 2nd ed., vol. III (Edmonton: Hurtig, 1988), 1457.

4 Elections British Columbia & the Legislative Library under the direction of Harry M. Goldberg, chief electoral officer & registrar of voters, *Electoral History of British Columbia 1871–1986* (1988). All subsequent election dates and results have been taken from this reference.

5 "Canada's Only Indian MLA Learns of Victory," *Prince Rupert Daily News,* July 6, 1949.

6 "Indian Greeting to Madam Speaker," *Vancouver Daily Province,* February 15, 1950, 1.

7 Ibid.

8 "Legislature Members Roar Approval as Indian MLA Makes First Speech," *Daily Colonist*, February 24, 1950.

9 Frank Calder, Scrapbook #1.

10 "Native Member Proposes Indians' Bill of Rights," *Victoria Times*, February 24, 1950.

11 "Wismer Scored for Discrimination Stand," *Vancouver Sun*, March 31, 1950.

12 Unpublished diary of missionaries at Greenville.

13 "'Clean Own Backyard First' Says Indian MLA," *Vancouver Province*, February 18, 1955.

14 "Indians, Whites Unite," *Prince Rupert Daily News*, June 1950, 1.

15 "Over 200 Delegates Pour into Victoria for Compensation," *The Fisherman*, March 11, 1952.

16 Government of Canada, Canadian Crown, Her Majesty Queen Elizabeth II. Online at canadiancrown.gc.ca (accessed February 8, 2009).

17 Jim Nesbit, "Good Things Come in Short Speeches," *Vancouver News Herald*, March 14, 1953.

18 "Political Roundup," *Daily News*, June 1, 1953.

CHAPTER 4: The Legislature, 1953–1956 (pp. 37–46)

1 Celia Haig-Brown, *Resistance and Renewal: Surviving the Indian Residential School* (Vancouver: Tillicum Library, 1988), 119.

2 Paul Tennant, *Aboriginal Peoples and Politics: The Indian Land Question in British Columbia, 1849–1989* (Vancouver, UBC Press, 1990), 121.

3 "The Mysterious Death of Peter Verigin," online at doukhobor.org/Han nant.htm (accessed Sept. 19, 2009).

4 "Indian Here Before Doukhobors," *Victoria Daily Times,* October 1, 1953, 30.

5 "Why Not an Indian Senator?" *Vancouver News Herald,* October 5, 1953.

6 "Gladstone Appointed to Canadian Senate," *The Canadian Encyclopedia,* 2nd ed., vol. II (Edmonton: Hurtig, 1988), 904.

7 *Prince Rupert Daily News,* December 4, 1958, 1, 7.

8 "Indian Fears 'Dirty Deal' on British Columbia," *Vancouver Sun,* March 26, 1954.

9 "QCA Officials Propose British Columbia Air Ambulance Line," *Vancouver Sun,* February 26, 1953.

10 "New Provincial Museum Asked by CCF Member," *Victoria Daily Times,* March 16, 1954, 2.

11 "'Cinderella' Comes to the Ball and Stays Past Midnight," *Vancouver Province,* January 19, 1956.

12 "Nishgas Take Long Step toward Liquor Rights," *The Native Voice,* December 1960, n.p.

CHAPTER 5: The Legislature, 1956–1963 (pp. 47–55)

1 "Calder Scores Indian Affairs Inaction Policy," *The Native Voice,* February 1956.

2 Ibid.

3 "National Congress of Canadian Indians: Progressive Powwow," *The Native Voice,* January 1954, 2–33.

4 "Brief to Skeena Salmon Management Committee," *The Fisherman,* February 20, 1959.

5 "Nass Natives Urge Basic Three Day Fishing Week," *The Fisherman,* February 20, 1959.

6 "Protect Salmon in Mid Pacific: Give Fleet More Time," *The Fisherman,* February 20, 1959.

7 "Campaign flyer for Atlin," *CCF News* (CCF Campaign Committee, 1960).

8 "New Approach Needed for Indians in Cities," *Vancouver Province*, January 31, 1963, 3.

9 "New Exit from the Teepee," *Victoria Daily Times*, February 13, 1961, 4.

10 J.V. Powell, "Chinook Jargon," in *The Canadian Encyclopedia,* 2nd ed., vol. 1 (Edmonton: Hurtig, 1988), 417. The word came from the Chinook First Nation that lived along the Columbia and Willamette rivers. They had been encountered by overland European traders in the late 1700s. Profitable trade soon extended to the Nootka, Nisga'a, Haida, Tshimshan and other First Nations. Communication was difficult because each First Nation spoke a different language, so Chinookan, commonly called Chinook, was used. The language varied somewhat from place to place, even adding some Chinese words at times. Scholars have estimated that Chinook was composed of 30 percent Chinook, 20 percent Nootka, 20 percent English, 20 percent French and 10 percent new words, such as "saltchuck" and "skookum." First Nations people sometimes used Chinook when trading with each other, and many children learned the language.

11 "North-south Discrimination," *Prince Rupert Daily News*, August 16, 1963.

12 "Bill of Rights Move by CCF Defeated by Government," *Vancouver Province*, March 24, 1961.

13 "I'm Broke – MLA Says," *Victoria Daily Times*, January 3, 1963.

14 "'End Winter Isolation,' MLA Asks," *Victoria Daily Times,* February 14, 1963, 23.

15 "New Democratic Party," in *The Canadian Encyclopedia* (Toronto: McClelland & Stewart, 2000).

CHAPTER 6: The Legislature, 1963–1966 (pp. 56–64)

1 "$4 Million Reported Price Likely in Power Takeover," *Prince Rupert Daily News,* February 13, 1964.

2 "Coast Highway to be Completed," *Yukon Daily News,* May 24, 1966.

3 Ministry of Public Safety and Solicitor General, Emergency Social Services, online at ess.bc.ca/history_bc.htm (accessed July 19, 2009).

4 "Disaster Teams Urged by Calder," *Victoria Daily Times*, January 27, 1965, 30.

5 Murray Lundberg, "Death Came Silently: The Granduc Mine Disaster," online at explorenorth.com/library/yafeatures/granduc.html (accessed July 20, 2009).

6 "Nishga Want Timber Supply for Future of Own Logging," *Prince Rupert Daily News*, April 21, 1964.

7 Pat Carney, "Timber-Conscious Tribe Means Business," *Vancouver Province,* April 21, 1964.

8 "Indian MLA Hails Hunting Decision," *Prince Rupert Daily News*, March 5, 1964.

9 "Indian Development Board Proposed by Frank Calder," *Vancouver Province, Victoria Bureau,* March 25, 1965, 7.

10 "Take Over Fisheries Control," *Vancouver Province,* February 17, 1966.

11 Jack Fry, "Socred Trio Oppose New Ridings," *Daily Colonist,* March 9, 1966.

12 "Calder in Battle with Fellow MLAs," *Prince Rupert Daily News*, November 30, 1965.

CHAPTER 7: Housing and the Legislature, 1966–1967 (pp. 65–72)

1 "Dent, Calder Hit Trail," *Vancouver Sun,* November 21, 1966.

2 "International Talks Urged to Protect Pacific Fishing," *Vancouver Sun,* October 20, 1970.

3 "Housing Aid Now $7000 for Indians," *Prince Rupert Daily News,* November 26, 1966.

4 Veterans Affairs Canada, online at veterans.gc.ca (accessed May 2008).

5 "Nass Needs Magistrate," *Prince Rupert Daily News,* November 4, 1968.

CHAPTER 8: Canada's Centennial Year and the Legislature, 1967–1969 (pp. 73–81)

1 "NDPers Praised by Liberal," *Victoria Times,* February 19, 1967.

2 "Indians Across Area Plan Longhouse," *Prince Rupert Daily News*, November 13, 1964.

3 Susan Marsden, Registrar of the Museum of Northern British Columbia, interview by author, May 29, 2011.

4 "Latest Indian Proposal Wins Calder's Praise," *Vancouver Province,* February 27, 1967.

5 "Housing, Health Needs Urgent: Land Rights Top Issue for Nisga'a," *The Fisherman,* November 3, 1967.

6 *Time Immemorial,* film directed by Hugh Brody, as part of the series *As Long as the Rivers Flow* (Tamarak Productions, National Film Board of Canada, 1991).

7 "Big Five Fail to Carry Indian Vote," *The Native Voice,* February 3, 1968.

8 "Superport Foreshore Rights Worry Indians," *Vancouver Province,* February 21, 1968.

9 "Berger Charges RCMP Brutality Against Indians," *Vancouver Province*, March 1968.

10 "Indian 'Prejudice' Study Slated," *Vancouver Province*, March 13, 1969.

11 "Labour Unions Told to Admit Indians," *Victoria Colonist*, February 13, 1971.

CHAPTER 9: BC Land Title Court Cases and the Legislature, 1969–1972 (pp. 82–90)

1 "British Columbia Indians Lose Court Land Battle," *Vancouver Province*, October 21, 1969.

2 Harry Hawthorn, ed., *A Survey of the Contemporary Indians of Canada: Economic, Political, Educational Needs and Policies* (Ottawa: Queen's Printer Press, 1966–1967), online at caid.ca/HawRep1a1966.pdf (accessed February 1, 2013).

3 "West Coast MLA Lauds Indian White Paper," *Montreal Star,* September 24, 1969.

4 "Talks Secret Claims Calder," *Victoria Times,* February 11, 1970.

5 Alex Rose, *Spirit Dance at Meziadin: Joseph Gosnell and the White Paper,* (Madeira Park: Harbour Publishing, 2001), 101–102.

6 "Calder Attacks Labour Leader Hayne," *Prince Rupert Daily News,* January 27, 1971.

7 "NDP Executive Rebukes Calder," *Vancouver Sun*, February 3, 1971.

8 "Calder Charge Denied," *Vancouver Province*, January 28, 1971.

9 Hamar Foster, with Heather Raven & Jeremy Webber, *Let Right Be Done: Aboriginal Title, the Calder Case and the Future of Indigenous Rights* (Vancouver: UBC Press, 2007), 62.

10 "Calder Honoured: Fourteenth Annual Tribal Council in Canyon City," *The Native Voice, Vol. 2, No. 3,* March, 1972.

11 "Correspondence Studies 'Stink' Claims Calder," *Vancouver Province,* March 11, 1971.

CHAPTER 10: The Calder Case, 1971–1973 (pp. 91–98)

1 Hamar Foster, with Heather Raven & Jeremy Webber, *Let Right Be Done: Aboriginal Title, the Calder Case and the Future of Indigenous Rights* (Vancouver: UBC Press, 2007), 224.

2 "This Land is Our Land," *Vancouver Province,* September 28, 1967.

3 Hamar Foster, with Heather Raven & Jeremy Webber, *Let Right Be Done: Aboriginal Title, the Calder Case and the Future of Indigenous Rights* (Vancouver: UBC Press, 2007), 129.

4 Robert MacRae, Anglican Archdeacon, interview by author, August 3, 2011.

5 John Becker, "Tangled Reconciliations: The Anglican Church and the Nisga'a of British Columbia," *American Ethnologist* 25, no. 3, (1998): 433 – 451.

6 Hamar Foster, with Heather Raven & Jeremy Webber, *Let Right Be Done: Aboriginal Title, the Calder Case and the Future of Indigenous Rights* (Vancouver: UBC Press, 2007), 36.

7 Barry M. Gough, *Gunboat Frontier: British Maritime Authority and Northwest Coast Indians, 1846–90* (Vancouver: UBC Press, 1984), 190.

8 Thomas H. Randall, *The Path of Destiny: Canada from British Conquest to Home Rule* (Toronto: Doubleday, 1957), 151, 155–156.

9 "Totem-pole Land," *Daily Colonist,* March 16, 1952.

10 Hamar Foster, with Heather Raven & Jeremy Webber, *Let Right Be Done: Aboriginal Title, the Calder Case and the Future of Indigenous Rights* (Vancouver: UBC Press, 2007), 52.

11 Thomas R. Berger, "The Nisga'a Odyssey," *One Man's Justice: A Life in the Law* (Vancouver: Douglas & McIntyre, 2002), 125.

12 Hamar Foster, 47, 59.

13 Ibid., 170.

CHAPTER 11: The Legislature, 1972–1973 (pp. 99–110)

1 Kathryn Hazel, "Calder's Appointment Blasted," *Daily Colonist,* September 21,1972.

2 "NDP Program for Northern Area Outlined by Two Leaders in Stewart," *Prince Rupert Daily News*, August 8, 1972, 5.

3 "Frank Announces a Program for the North with Barrett," (partial newspaper article found in Frank Calder, Scrapbook #4).

4 "Reunion Attracts 150," *The Chilliwack Progress*, October 25, 1972.

5 Paul Moss, "No 'Bureaucracy' for Calder," *Victoria Times*, April 5, 1973.

6 "Equal Salary Claim Hinted by Calder," *Vancouver Sun*, April 5, 1973.

7 "AG Says Native Land Claims are in Federal Jurisdiction," *Prince Rupert Daily News*, June 8, 1973.

8 "Indian Claim Moves Sought," *Daily Colonist*, March 7, 1973, 40.

9 Barbara McClintock, "Barrett Sacks Calder: Lost Confidence," *Daily Colonist*, August 1, 1973.
10 Iain Hunter, "Was Calder Too Close to Liberals?" *Victoria Times*, August 9, 1973.
11 Jim Hume, "Hard Times Await New Crop of MLAs," *Times Colonist*, June 21, 2009, D11.
12 "Even Foes Agree on 200-Mile Limit," *Prince Rupert Daily News*, June 8, 1973.
13 *"Bill 93 – Emergency Health Services 3,"* Archived Journals of the Legislative Assembly Journal from 1851–1991, Index to Journals, Session 1974/75, One Hundred & Sixth Volumes. R.206 R.A. 212, online at http://test. archives.leg.bc.ca/ (accessed Nov. 5, 2009).

CHAPTER 12: Frank Proposes (pp. 111–117)

1 Tamaki Calder's account of her meeting and developing relationship with Frank, as recorded in private interviews with the author, January to April 2009.

CHAPTER 13: Marriage (pp. 118–132)

1 *Hansard,* February 26, 1975, afternoon sitting.
2 Ibid.
3 *The Unforgettable Winston Churchill: Giant of the Century* (New York: *Time Life* Inc., 1965), 38, 42.

CHAPTER 14: The Legislature, 1976–1979 (pp. 133–143)

1 "Keio Woman Graduate Marries Indian chief," film by Tokyo Broadcasting System, 1977.
2 "Gosnell" is the name of a prominent Nisga'a family. James (Jimmy) Gosnell succeeded Frank as president of the Nisga'a Council. Eli Gosnell was a famous carver, and Chief Joseph Gosnell was a negotiator of the Nisga'a Treaty. He received an honorary doctorate for his work and was known as Dr. Joseph Gosnell.
3 *Citizens Plus: The Nisga'a People of the Nass River Valley in Northwestern British Columbia,* rev ed. (New Aiyansh, British Columbia: The Nisga'a Tribal Council, 1980).
4 William W. Fitzhugh & Chisato O. Dubreuil, eds., *Ainu: Spirit of a Northern People* (Seattle: U of Washington Press, 2001).

CHAPTER 15: In Retirement, 1980–2000 (pp. 144–154)

1 Keith Baldrey, "Reprise of Operation Solidarity Unlikely," online at canada. com/northshorenews/news/story.html?id=6492e07d-8271-4ffc-a2cb-02ed 06537eee (accessed June 20, 2009).
2 Marius Barbeau, *Haida Myths* (Ottawa: Queens Printer, 1953), 561.
3 Owe Ka Tahpqwit, as Mt. Ararat is known in the Nisga'a language.
4 Story confirmed by Phillip Calder.

CHAPTER 16: The Nisga'a Treaty, 1991–2000 (pp. 155–164)

1 William Rayner, *Scandal!!: 130 Years of Damnable Deeds in Canada's Lotus Land* (Nanoose Bay, BC: Heritage House, 2001) 68–75.
2 Ibid., 20.
3 Ibid., 204.
4 *Hansard*, Aug. 4, 1998, 3rd session of the 36th Legislature.
5 The Nisga'a Exhibition at the Royal British Columbia Museum, June 2008.
6 The Nisga'a Final Agreement, prepared by Mary C. Hurley Law and Government Division, February 9, 1999, revised September 24, 2001: 10 of 16.
7 *Hansard*, December 1, 1998, 3rd session of the 36th Legislature.
8 William Rayner, *Scandal!!: 130 Years of Damnable Deeds in Canada's Lotus Land* (Nanoose Bay, BC: Heritage House, 2001), 68–75.
9 *Hansard,* April 21, 1999, 1st. session of the 37th Legislature.
10 Ibid., April 22, 1999.
11 Michael Smyth, "Calder a Man of Principle," *Vancouver Province*, April 23, 1999.
12 "Nisga'a Lisims Government," online at nisgaalisims.ca (accessed October 28, 2008).

CHAPTER 17: He Will Move that Mountain (pp. 165–174)

1 Tamaki Calder's poem as printed in Frank's funeral Order of Service.
2 Jim Hume, "Chief of Chiefs," *Times Colonist*, November 17, 2006, D7.

ABOUT THE AUTHOR

Joan Harper grew up listening to her father's tales of the north, of his time trapping and fishing and working with First Nations people. From the beginning she was attracted to Frank Calder, his Nisga'a heritage and his early life as a boy on the Nass River. Joan's professional life included work in library education at the Vancouver School Board and at the University of BC, teaching library science. Shortly after Frank's death she met Frank's wife, Tamaki Calder, who asked her to write Frank's biography. Tamaki gave her unlimited access to Frank's papers, which Joan augmented with extensive archival research and interviews with Frank's friends, his colleagues and in particular with his extended family. Joan resides with her husband in Sechelt, BC.

INDEX